KU-464-781

Aberdeenshire
C O U N C I L

Aberdeenshire Libraries
www.aberdeenshire.gov.uk/libraries
Renewals Hotline 01224 661511

1 9 MAR 2015

0 8 JAN 2016

ABERDEENSHIRE
LIBRARIES

WITHDRAWN
FROM LIBRARY

BURKE,
HERBS

Aberdeenshire

3127254

Growing & Using
Herbs
& spices

DON BURKE

ABERDEENSHIRE LIBRARIES	
3127254	
Bertrams	21/01/2014
635.7	£14.99

First published in 2013 by
New Holland Publishers Pty Ltd
London • Sydney • Cape Town • Auckland

Garfield House 86–88 Edgware Road London W2 2EA United Kingdom
1/66 Gibbes Street Chatswood NSW 2067 Australia
Wembley Square First Floor Solan Road Gardens Cape Town 8001 South Africa
218 Lake Road Northcote Auckland New Zealand

www.newhollandpublishers.com

Copyright © 2013 New Holland Publishers
Copyright © 2013 in text: Don Burke
Copyright © 2013 in images: recipe images NHIL, all other images © CTC Productions 2013

All rights reserved. No part of this publication may be reproduced, stored in a retrieval system or transmitted, in any form or by any means, electronic, mechanical, photocopying, recording or otherwise, without the prior written permission of the publishers and copyright holders.

A record of this book is held at the British Library and the National Library of Australia

ISBN 9781921517303

Publisher: Fiona Schultz
Project editor: Jodi De Vantier
Editorial consultant: Jamie McIlwraith, Juno Creative Services
Production coordinator: Chris Burke
Designer: Tracy Loughlin
Design consultant: Zora Regulic
Principal photographer: Brent Wilson
Additional photography: Seán van Doornum
Illustrations: Pamela Horsnell, Juno Creative Services pages: 26, 30, 42, 54, 56, 58, 82, 96, 106, 116, 124, 128, 136, 144, 154, 168, 178, 190, 204, 206, 214, 216, 218, 226, 246, 258, 272, 274, 290, 294. All others NHIL UK.
Production director: Olga Dementiev
Printer: Toppan Leefung Printing Ltd (China)

10 9 8 7 6 5 4 3 2 1

Keep up with New Holland Publishers on Facebook http://www.facebook.com/NewHollandPublishers

With thanks to:
Jamie McIlwraith for his sharp mind, tireless support and boundless enthusiasm, without whom this book would not be possible. Pamela Horsnell for her wonderful botanical illustrations. Special thanks also to Elizabeth Swane, Julie McCrory, Seán van Doornum and the ever-resourceful photographer Brent Wilson.

Growing & Using Herbs & spices

DON BURKE

Contents

Herbs & spices — 7
Flavour saviours — 7
Practicalities — 7

Planning a herb garden — 8
Going to bed — 8
The soil — 9
Odd man out — 9
Mediterraneans — 9
Pests & diseases — 9

Medicinal & mythical uses of herbs — 10
Nonsense V science — 10
Proven benefits — 10

Fresh is best! — 11
Getting started — 11
Herbs in pots — 11
Tips & tricks — 12
Indoor gardens — 12
Drying herbs — 13
Freezing herbs — 13
In the kitchen — 13
Creative teas — 14

Herbs & Spices
listed from A to Y — 16–301

Index of scientific names — 302
Index of common names — 303
Index of recipes — 304

Herbs & spices

Herbs are by far the best and easiest of all edible plants to grow. They are also the most useful edible plant group. For the purposes of this book, HERBS are plants that produce leaves that we can use in food and drink flavouring, or in medicines or perfumes.

They are those wonderful plants like coriander, mint or basil. We will also include leaves from trees like the tea plant and the lemon-scented myrtle.

SPICES are similar products made from non-leafy plant parts like bark, fruit, seeds, roots and even pollen (eg, saffron, the world's most expensive spice). Usually they are sold dried out. Since we are only looking at spices that can be grown and eaten at home, the spice list is fairly short. Most spices simply can't be grown easily at home: can you imagine collecting crocus flowers to shake out the pollen to make saffron! Or removing the bark from a cinnamon tree to make cinnamon?

Flavour saviours

In days gone by, food was often pretty rancid. Refrigerators and freezers simply didn't exist. For much of the year, especially in the colder months, most good foods were out of season. This is why people grew strange foods like turnips and parsnips, and even better foods like carrots, beetroot, apples, pears, pumpkins, onions, garlic and various nuts: all of these foods (if you can call parsnips food) store very well without a refrigerator over winter.

To disguise the awful taste of semi-rotten or just plain boring food, people used herbs and spices. These flavour-improvers were also used in soups to improve their appeal. Remember that many soups and stews were kept boiling for weeks or months to stop the food from going off. The very opposite of a refrigerator, but producing the same effect: long-term food preservation. This is precisely what minestrone soup was – a soup that was kept hot and eaten over a long period and topped up with new ingredients every day or two.

Perhaps the ultimate in the use of food flavouring sauces are those controlled by the Sauce Police at Japanese restaurants. This dish goes with that sauce! No, not this one, that one! While you can argue that there are some good reasons to match up the sauces as instructed, fellow anarchists might wish to make their own choices; this book is written for you. In the privacy of your own home you can even experiment with chocolate sauce mixed with chilli. This is a major Mexican triumph in dishes such as Mole Poblano – chicken in a chilli and chocolate sauce.

Practicalities

You only need small amounts of herbs and spices, so the large bunches sold at supermarkets are often poor value. You just don't need that much. On top of that,

FRESH is absolutely essential with herbs and spices. A great idea is to grow useful herbs like various mints, basil, chives, rosemary, coriander and parsley in attractive terracotta pots and place them on the table when you have guests over for dinner. Talk about fresh!

Herbs are like fingernails – you must trim them often otherwise they are useless. Old, rank growth on herbs tastes bad, so give your herbs a haircut every few weeks: if you can't use the herbs at the time, dry the branches out under the house or in a protected, shady spot and use them later.

After you master the basic herbs, we strongly recommend trying out specialised herbs that go with particular types of cooking. Balinese herbs like galangal go very well with Indonesian food like Prahok with pork belly. Your friends will never forget the night…

Planning a herb garden

One rule dominates herb garden design. It must be right outside the back or front door. Or better still, in a pot on the table. The basic necessity is to grab and go.

As with vegetable gardens, fruit tree orchards and old celebrities, herb gardens must be in the full glare of the sun. That is, eight hours of sun each day. Herbs are like Boy George's Karma Chameleon: they COME & GO. So you must plan the garden to cope with bare, dead or scruffy areas, or perhaps areas that are neither one thing nor another.

The best solution is to create a geometrical design that looks good even if the star performers are old and bedraggled. This can be as simple as a row of colourful pots or even terracotta pots filled with herbs. Or it could be a parterre garden: this is a fancy word for a geometrically interesting collection of smallish garden plots. It could be rows of plots in the shape of squares, rectangles or triangles in brick pavers or in concrete; all filled with herbs. This will look good even when everything is mostly dead in winter – due to the geometry.

A row of windowsill pots of herbs looks excellent, but you must have pots no smaller in diameter than 20cm/8in and easy access for watering. Pots on windowsills tend to overcook in the baking sun, so basic boring maintenance is paramount.

It pays to prepare the soil very well. Dig in coarse sand and lots of manure or compost. There is no law anywhere in the world that says that you can't mix pretty flowers with your herbs as well. Herb gardens can look very pretty! Mix in pest-repelling plants like dwarf marigolds and pyrethrum daisies too. A mulch of lucerne hay or pea straw will create the farmyard chicken-nest feel and improve the soil out of sight as well.

Going to bed

As winter approaches your herb garden will go to bed: to sleep. Herbs like basil and chillies will go to God (unless you live in tropical areas). Others will go dormant to re-emerge in spring. Some people grow basil indoors in sunny windows or even in warm, protected courtyards over winter.

Renewal is the key concept to embrace with herb gardens. Some herbs are quick fizzers: coriander will bolt to seed and death during the warm months. So, avoid planting it during summer unless you are growing it mostly for seeds and/or the root. If it is the leaves that you want, coriander is best planted during the cooler months.

This coming and going is the rhythm of the herb garden.

The soil

A slightly raised garden bed is best for all plants all of the time – whether they are herbs or not. If the soil is raised about 15–20cm/6–8in above the surrounding ground, the bases of the plants will be protected from inundation during periods of heavy rain. This protects the plants from root rot and other diseases. By digging coarse sand and compost or manure into the soil, the area will finish up raised without you having to worry about it.

Odd man out

But there is always an odd man out: most varieties of mint love a damp position. Nonetheless, mint grows very well in a raised garden bed or in a pot as long as it gets plenty of water. Mint never flourishes unless it gets a lot of water.

Mediterraneans

Another odd group are the Mediterranean plants like rosemary, lavender, thyme and sage. All of these plants like lime as they originate on coasts or on bleak, windy islands in the Mediterranean Sea where the soil is mostly broken up lumps of limestone. Lavender in particular needs lime to do well. This also applies to fruiting fig and olive trees. So, add no less than one large handful of lime to each square metre (or square yard) of ground where you are to grow any of these plants.

The idea is to have your specialised limestone plot or plots in your herb garden. In these, you rotate the above-listed group of lime-lovers. All Mediterranean plants also strongly prefer very well-drained soils with little organic matter (ie, no added compost or manure) and they detest too much fertiliser. Over-fertilising may cause rapid growth that is prone to fungal dieback of stems and branches.

To sum up, Mediterranean plants belong to the "treat 'em mean and keep 'em keen" brigade of plants. Treating these plants well with lots of watering in summer and lots of fertiliser and compost will almost certainly lead to trouble sooner or later.

Pests & diseases

In general, most herbs get very few pests or diseases since the strong smell or flavour of herbs is their natural defence against these problems. This explains why herbs are very useful for human health. The flavoursome and/or odorous parts of herbs tend to help the fight against parasites and diseases in people.

Medicinal & mythical uses of herbs

Many herbs really are helpful against all sorts of human complaints and problems. They have been used for this purpose for thousands of years. Since there is now clear proof that many wild animals use plants and minerals for specific health issues, it is certain that the use of such health-giving plants and minerals goes back millions of years; long before human beings evolved on Earth. One classic use of herbs occurs in wild horses – research has shown that horses precisely balance their diets and health with all sorts of wild herbage. So-called improved pastures are, in fact, not very good for grazing animals. Another classic study is of Amazonian parrots that travel long distances to eat clay soil from clay-banks to neutralise the poisons such as strychnine, quinine and tannic acids in their diet of various fruits. These "poisons", however, help rid the birds' intestines of parasites.

Nonsense V science

That having been said, much of the herbal medicine in older herbal books is simply nonsense. If you read Culpepper (1616-1654) – the best-known of the foundation herbalists – much of the uses for herbs reflect the weird hang-ups of the day. He is mired in flatulence, women's periods, venereal diseases, hemorrhoids and provoking urine. He rarely strays far from the nether regions. Perhaps the best indication of the practicality of his work is that he only lived to 38!

But there is hope! The messiah is the late Dr Varro Tyler (1926-2001), former dean of the colleges of Pharmacy and Pharmaceutical Sciences at Purdue University in the USA. He is by far the best authority on what herbs REALLY DO. He conducted and gathered the best scientific studies on most herbs from around the world and published them in his excellent book *Tyler's Honest Herbal*. It is out of print, but you can get second-hand copies from Amazon. We strongly recommend his books and wish to point out that he lived to the age of 75, about twice the lifespan of Culpepper.

Much of our health information comes from *Tyler's Honest Herbal*. Since Tyler's death, Wikipedia is a very useful modern source of herbal information. Beware internet pseudo-science and other bogus sources of information.

Proven benefits

There is still much misleading information out there about herbs and, in general, herbal products are not governed by the strict rules of proven efficacy that mainstream medicines are required to comply with.

Nonetheless, garlic has been scientifically proven to be an excellent antibiotic, as has honey. It is worth noting that for garlic to work it must be smelly: refinement destroys the antibiotic properties in it. Garlic can also be useful for protection against coronary thrombosis and stroke. We strongly suggest that you consult your Doctor about all significant health issues though. The antibiotics in honey have made it an excellent product to dip plant cuttings into. Honey fights the decay that the exposed cut end of the cuttings often suffer – that is, it increases your strike rate with the cuttings.

Curries have been shown to delay the onset of dementia. Perhaps the 1.3 billion people in India will inherit the world as they age well! Consider how good Cliff Richard looks at 73! He was born in Lucknow, India in 1940, and yes, he is Anglo-Indian. In the meantime eat lots of curries and turmeric.

Herbs and spices can become an excellent part of your health regime and they can spark up the flavour of your food as well.

Fresh is best!

Getting started

Which herbs and spices should you grow? It's up to you, as it all depends on the food you like to eat now, or want to eat from now on.

Each plant entry inside this book includes growing tips for that herb or spice. These will tell you the climate that each plant likes, how big it grows, when to plant it and how to care for it. If it sounds like it could grow in your garden, on your balcony, or inside, then have a go at growing it.

Sometimes our growing tips will tell you not to bother trying to grow some plants. For example, cloves: unless you're on a steamy tropical island located close to the equator don't even think about attempting to grow this amazing, exotic spice tree. The same goes for fragrant tropical vanilla orchids: it's just too difficult to try growing and processing this climbing orchid vine at home.

Herbs in pots

Lots of people grow some herbs in pots, often because they can locate pots just outside their kitchen door, where they are easy to get to. Our herb and spice listings will tell you whether you can grow that plant in pots. Here's our five top tips for growing herbs in pots.

1. As for pot sizes, the bigger the better – but if you start with one at least 20cm (8in) across and grow the one type of herb in it, that should work very well. If you want to grow a few herbs together in the one pot (and that can look fabulous), make sure it is a big one, such as a trough, and give each herb room to spread – don't overcrowd it.

2. Use a good quality potting mix. Don't put ordinary garden soil in pots, it's too heavy and dense and most herbs won't grow in it at all. Special potting mixes formulated for herbs are available.

3. Don't sit your pots in puddles of water. Sure, it's fine to put a saucer under a pot to catch the excess water that drains out after watering, but don't leave the water there as it can cause plants to rot from the bottom up. We prefer to sit our potted herbs up on pot feet, so all the excess water drains away.

4. Use slow-release fertilisers. These pellets are designed to provide a gentle trickle of food into the potting mix over a long period, and that's ideal for herbs and other potted plants.

5. Keep clipping back your potted herbs, whether you need the leaves for the kitchen or not. This keeps plants bushy and attractive, and the new growth of foliage is the best stuff to use when harvesting. Old leaves don't taste as nice as young ones.

Tips & tricks

Happy groups: some herbs love regular watering and fertiliser (eg, parsley, basil, coriander, chives, dill), and other herbs hate too much water and fertiliser (eg, thyme, sage and rosemary) so when planting out a pot or a herb bed, try to create 'groupings' of herbs which like the same amount of water and fertiliser.

Plant heights: remember that some herbs grow much taller than others, so plant the low-growing herbs (like parsley and chives) at the front of your herb bed, and the tall-growing herbs (like rosemary) at the back of the bed, with the medium-height herbs (like basil and tarragon) in the middle of the bed.

Short-lived herbs: bear in mind that some herb and spice plants only live for one year, or in some cases just a few months. Coriander, dill and basil, for example, usually only live for a few months at best. Parsley can live a bit longer, but 18 months is the most you can expect, and often less than a year is typical. Most chilli plants last about one year, although some types will soldier on. Many of these short-lived herbs are called 'annuals', meaning they live out their life-cycle in the space of just one year. So, in your herb garden, plan on replanting these at least once a year.

Long-lived herbs: other herb and spice plants are there to enjoy a long stay in your garden, some for many years. Examples include small growing plants such as thyme, sage, oregano and mint, plus shrubs such as lavender and rosemary, and trees such as the curry leaf, lemon myrtle and bay leaf trees.

Indoor gardens

Yes, of course you can grow herbs indoors. It's not as easy as growing them outdoors, but it can be done (and your guests will be impressed).

As most herbs love sunshine, try to grow your potted herbs on a sunny windowsill or at least in a sunny room (but never forget to water them, as it can hot there on summer days in particular).

Pick your indoor herbs regularly, even if you don't need the leaves for the kitchen, to keep them bushy.

Don't let potted indoor herbs sit in puddles of water, either. Use a saucer to catch the water that drains out, then throw that excess water away.

Grow herbs which will cope with less than perfect sunshine. Great choices for indoor herb gardens are mint and chervil (which both like a bit of shade, anyway) and parsley (which copes with partial sun fairly well).

Drying herbs

This is a lovely skill to learn, and it's easy. To dry herbs, cut a bunch of the one herb, tie some string around the base of the bunch and hang it up in a dry, airy spot (doesn't have to be sunny) for a week or more (drying times will vary with the herb and your climate) until fully dry (the leaves will be crumbly).

Store dried herbs in airtight jars for use in the kitchen. Bunches of dried herbs (and flowers) can also be a lovely home-made decoration around the house, and some of them, such as lavender, can give off a wonderful aroma.

Good candidates for dried herbs include: bay leaves, lemon myrtle leaves, lavender, marjoram, oregano, rosemary, sage and thyme.

Freezing herbs

Some herbs freeze well – examples include parsley, chives, basil, tarragon, chervil and dill. One good way to freeze them is to chop each herb finely, place as much as you can in an ice-cube tray and top this with water, then freeze. When you need that herb in cooking, place the whole ice-cube in the pot. Remember to label the ice-cube trays so you know which herb is which.

In the kitchen

Most good cooks prefer to use fresh herbs in the kitchen, but some dried herbs are still very useful. That's the big advantage of growing herbs at home: there's nothing fresher, and that freshly harvested herb flavour really makes a difference to every dish.

All herbs should be washed before use, to remove airborne dust and other contaminants. Just follow the recipe suggestions for when to add the herbs to the pot. Some will say to add freshly chopped herbs just before serving, others will tell you to toss the herbs into the pot right at the beginning of cooking. Both methods can work perfectly well, depending on the herb used and the other ingredients.

As you cook with fresh herbs, you'll learn that some have a powerful flavour – such as rosemary and sage – so don't add too much, and just stick to the recipe for starters. Other herbs have a milder flavour – such as parsley and chervil, so feel free to add a bit more if your tastebuds tell you extra flavour is needed.

The rules regarding using spices in the kitchen are almost the opposite to those governing herbs: most cooks use dried spices (eg, cardamom, cinnamon, cloves, pepper, star anise, turmeric powder) but some fresh spices (eg, ginger, galangal) are essential. Sticking to the recipe is our best advice if you are a beginner with spices.

Creative teas

You'll notice in our book that many listings for herbs and spices include tips on using each one for making tea. You've probably already enjoyed cups of mint tea but have you tried cardamom tea yet?

The key thing to remember with using herbs or spices in making teas is that the plants have never been sprayed with insecticides, which could be harmful to your health. Fortunately, most herbs are very pest and disease resistant, and so need little or no spraying. If you grow your own herbs at home, and don't use sprays, then there is nothing to worry about. However, if buying herbs to use in making teas, please ask if these herbs have been organically grown, without the use of pesticides. If the shopkeeper is unsure, or says no, don't risk it.

Herbs and spices are sometimes used to make a cup of tea on their own, but they are more often used in combination with other herbs and spices (such as in the various Indian chai blends) or to flavour traditional green or black teas.

If you're a committed tea experimenter, look for our entry on growing your own tea plants – *Camellia sinensis* – at home. These are the same plants grown in plantations in India, Sri Lanka and elsewhere, and these hardy plants can grow in a wide variety of gardens. They make wonderful clipped hedging plants (and save the clippings to dry and make a pot of green tea) and bring you as close as possible to the mysteries of growing, drying and creating your own signature cup of tea.

Fresh or dried? Just remember that when using fresh herbs you will need to add more to the pot, compared with using dried herbs. As a general guide, ¼ cup of fresh leaves is equivalent to 2 teaspoons of dried herbs.

Herbs
& Spices

Allspice

Pimenta dioica

This versatile spice not only has many names – Jamaica pepper, myrtle pepper and pimenta – it also has many flavours, spicy like cloves, warm like cinnamon, peppery too, hence the common name of 'allspice'. One key component of allspice is eugenol, the same active ingredient found in cloves. The spice itself is actually the dried berry (unripe fruit) of *Pimenta dioica*, a large, 10-18m/30–60ft tall tropical tree native to the Caribbean and Central America, with leaves which resemble those of the bay tree.

Growing basics: trees grow best in a tropical climate, and as they also grow quite tall are not commonly grown in domestic gardens, although they are not especially difficult to grow in the tropics and subtropics. However, both a male and female tree are required to produce berries. Fruits are picked when green and unripe then sun-dried, at which point they become the familiar brown berries about twice the size of a peppercorn.

In the kitchen: allspice is one of the classic pickling spices in European cuisine, and it's widely used in Caribbean and Central American cookery (it's a notable ingredient in jerk seasoning for grilled meats), but also is common in Middle-Eastern dishes. Its warm flavouring is found in many spice mixes to flavour sausages, as well as in cakes, biscuits and pastries. Many commercial sauces use allspice in the blend, so you probably consume more of it than you realise. It combines well at home with many vegetables, and other spices such as cloves, coriander, cumin, mace and pepper. It's best to buy whole dried berries and grind enough as the recipes require, as the already-ground spice loses flavour quite quickly. Keep dried berries in an air-tight jar in a cupboard.

Allspice tea: though it's not used on its own as a flavouring for tea, allspice as part of a blend of several spices is found in some Indian chai mixes.

Baked apples

Serves 4

4 large baking apples, cored
½ cup white wine or white grape juice
¼ cup honey
1 tablespoon ground cinnamon
¼ teaspoon allspice
1 teaspoon ground ginger
2 tablespoons raisins
3 teaspoons butter, melted

1 Preheat oven to 190°C/ 375°F.

2 Place the cored apples in a baking dish, then pour in the wine or grape juice. Mix the remaining ingredients in a bowl, then place a quarter of the mixture in the centre of each apple.

3 Place in the oven. Bake until tender, approximately 30–40 minutes. Baste apples with pan juices a few times while cooking. Serve warm.

Aloe vera

Aloe vera

One plant whose common name is also its botanical name is aloe vera (which is also known as **A. barbadensis**). This medicinal plant thrives as an indoor potted specimen in cooler climates and is a low-maintenance outdoor succulent in warm to hot, frost-free climates. In the garden, these plants can slowly spread from the base to form clumps 60-100cm/2-3ft high and wide, but many people would know it as a smaller potted indoor plant. Aloe veras can flower, sending up a tall spike covered in thin, bell-shaped orange, yellow or red flowers in late spring, summer or early autumn.

Growing basics: aloe vera can be grown from seed sown during late spring and summer in temperate zones, and at any time of year in subtropical and tropical zones. However, it's more commonly grown by taking an offset from the base of an existing plant and striking roots from this cutting in a sandy propagating mix. Leaving the cutting to dry out for a few days, prior to potting up, is recommended. Plants can be fed in spring with a liquid food, but overwatering is the cause of the death of most aloe veras, especially indoor plants. Aloes will grow in full sun to partial shade, and a free-draining soil or potting mix is essential.

Growing in pots: aloe vera is an ideal potted plant to grow indoors or outside in full sun to partial shade.

Using aloe vera: if you experience a cut or scratch in the garden, or a burn in the kitchen, after cleaning and disinfecting the wound as normal, break off a piece of aloe vera and apply the gel which exudes from the leaf to the affected area, to speed the healing process. Aloe vera is also used to treat eczema. Commercially, aloe vera is an ingredient in various hand creams, lotions and shampoos, but scientific tests cast doubt on whether the healing benefits of the gel from leaves are retained in all of these products. Special creams containing aloe vera gel, used for treating burns, work well. Aloe vera is purely a medicinal plant and has no uses in the kitchen.

Biblical aloe: the 'aloe' mentioned in the Bible is not aloe vera. It's an incense product made from fragrant aloe wood.

Amaranthus

Amaranthus spp.

The traditional gardener's names for this ornamental flowering plant are 'tassel flower' and 'love lies bleeding' (*Amaranthus caudatus*) but to Vietnamese cooks another very edible species of amaranthus is called rau den, in China it's en choy (or Chinese spinach) and in India, it's marsa. In some areas the plants grow as weeds (often called pigweed) which are harvested where they are found. Some amaranth plants are grown for their seeds/grains, others for their leaves, but in many other cases the plants, with their colourful foliage and flowers, are purely decorative, even if they might be edible. The common names for the amaranth grown as vegetables are red amaranth and green amaranth, and these could be any of *A. tricolor*, *A. oleraceus*, *A. dubins* or *A. spinosus*. Similarly, several species of amaranth are grown for their seeds, most notably *A. leucocarpus*.

Growing basics: amaranth is mostly an annual plant which grows quickly and easily from seed in both temperate and tropical climate zones in rich, well-drained soil in full sun. Sow seed in spring. Plants can reach 100-180cm/3.3-6ft tall and spread 60-80cm/2-2.5ft.

Picking tips: in many gardens whole plants are pulled up as needed, although picking individual leaves is also an option. To harvest seeds, plants are allowed to flower in summer, then seeds are harvested later, in autumn.

In the kitchen: think 'spinach' and you'll know how to cook and enjoy amaranth leaves. They're also used in the many Asian soups and stir-fry recipes requiring leafy greens. When shopping for amaranth, the plants sold with their roots still attached keep longer than those just sold as leaves. Whole plants will keep for about a week in the fridge. Before cooking, wash thoroughly then cut off and discard the roots. Amaranth seeds are cooked and eaten as a grain, and they were a traditional food of the ancient Incas and Aztecs of the Americas. Though not a true grain, amaranth seeds are treated as a protein-rich, nutritious cereal. All species of pet birds love amaranth and it is good for them.

Medicinal herbs: some species of amaranth, notably *A. hypochondriacus*, are grown as medicinal herbs which have a diuretic and laxative effect.

Pictured left: Redroot Pigweed, *Amaranthus retroflexus*

Amchoor

Mangifera indica

Also spelled amchur, this dried spice used in Indian cookery is made from mangoes (which is why it is sometimes labelled in shops as 'mango powder'). The mango tree itself is a common sight in many subtropical and tropical gardens, a broad-spreading 5–15m/16–50ft tall and 5–10m/16–33ft wide evergreen shade tree bearing crops of delicious, big, sweet, fruits coloured either green, yellow, orange or red. However, there are many different species of mango trees apart from the dessert mangoes, most notably those grown to produce mangoes which are harvested while still green and unripe for use as a vegetable for making salads or the production of amchoor.

Growing basics: mango trees do best in subtropical and tropical zones, but they can be grown in sheltered positions in warm, frost-free, temperate areas. In these cooler zones, trees will grow smaller and crops will take longer to ripen. Mangoes can be grown from a mango seed (in fact it's the only fruit tree on Earth that produces identical, cloned plants from seed). Mango trees need feeding in spring and summer with a complete plant food formulated for fruit trees. Regular watering and mulching ensures steady growth.

Making amchoor: after harvesting, the green mango is cut into slices and dried (either sun-dried or in special drying rooms). This is then processed further to create the powdered amchoor most cooks buy and use.

In the kitchen: amchoor provides a sour, acid taste to many dishes without the need to add liquid (in that sense, it's a substitute for tamarind, which is mostly added as a liquid). Amchoor's flavour is stronger than lemon juice, so just one teaspoon of amchoor is equivalent to three tablespoons of lemon juice. It's used in making a wide range of soups and stews, and combines particularly well with vegetables such as cauliflower, eggplant, beans, lentils, peas, okra and potatoes. It also blends well with spices such as chilli, cloves, coriander, cumin and ginger, and herbs such as coriander and mint. Amchoor is also used as a tenderising agent in marinades for grilled meats, poultry and fish, and its sourness is often added to chutneys. You can sometimes buy orange-brown slices of dried green mango which also have that sharp, sour taste. These are added to pickles, curries, dals and soups, but the amchoor slices are removed prior to serving.

Sour prawn (shrimp) curry

Serves 4

2 cups/1 pint coconut milk
1 teaspoon shrimp paste
2 tablespoons/1 oz Thai green curry paste
1 stalk lemongrass, finely chopped, or ½ teaspoon
    dried lemongrass, soaked in hot water until soft
2 fresh green chillies, chopped
1 tablespoon/½ oz ground cumin
1 tablespoon/½ oz ground coriander
500g/1 lb large uncooked prawns, shelled, deveined
    (leaving tails intact)
3 cucumbers, halved and sliced
115g/4 oz canned bamboo shoots, drained
1 tablespoon/½ oz amchoor (mango powder)
    or tamarind concentrate, dissolved in 3
    tablespoons/1½ oz hot water

1 Place the coconut milk, shrimp paste, curry paste, lemongrass, chillies, cumin and coriander in a slow cooker set on high and bring to a simmer. Stirring occasionally, cook for 1 hour.

2 Stir the prawns, cucumbers, bamboo shoots and amchoor mixture into the coconut milk mixture and cook, stirring occasionally, for 45 minutes or until the prawns are cooked.

3 Serve with steamed rice.

Bananas

Musa x *paradisiaca*

One major surprise for most people is the discovery that banana trees (*Musa* x *paradisiaca*) are classed as herbs – very large herbs grown for their fruits, yes, but they are herbs. And it's not just those delicious, healthy fruits which are useful in the kitchen. Banana leaves are the alfoil of the tropics, used for wrapping all kinds of cooked foods: fish, pork, vegetables, whether cooked in an oven, on a barbecue, in a steamer, or a roasting pit dug into the ground.

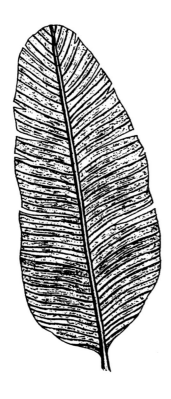

Growing basics: banana trees might be happiest in the hot, humid tropics (they're originally from India and South Asia) but they can be grown successfully in the subtropics and even in warm, temperate, frost-free zones. Generally, the cooler the climate the slower they grow and the slower the crops ripen. Bananas are grown from suckers taken from a parent plant. These suckers are planted year-round in the tropics, but in cooler and temperate areas plant them in late spring. After a sucker has produced fruit, it produces suckers around it, but it will not fruit again. Well-drained, fertile soil is a must, and regular applications of fertiliser will help, too.

Growing in pots: banana trees are too large to grow successfully in pots. However, there is an ornamental dwarf red banana plant (*Musa velutina*) which is well-suited to growing in pots, has interesting yellow flowers and red, seedy fruits. Other ornamental bananas include *M. ornata* (with purple bracts) and *M. zebrina* (with striped foliage), and the dwarf *M. acuminata*, with fragrant, edible fruit.

In the kitchen: banana leaves have long been used as wrappers for cooking foods in tropical climates. They are now more readily available in climate zones outside the tropics. While recipes are endless, the cooking method is to include the main food (eg, chicken, fish, pork) along with the herbs, spices, vegetables and other flavourings, wrap them all together in a few layers of banana leaves, tie up the bundle, and cook. A simpler method is to use banana leaves to create small, individual parcels for each serving (for example, fish with herbs and spices) and cook and serve these individually. The banana leaf is not edible, and is discarded once the food is unwrapped.

Varieties: there are many varieties of bananas available. Many are sweet, such as the widely-grown large 'Cavendish', and the smaller, sweeter 'Lady Fingers' and 'Sugar Banana' varieties. However, plantain bananas are not sweet, and form a very important vegetable crop in many tropical countries.

Health: banana fruits are rich in Vitamin C and potassium, and a moderate source of fibre and iron.

Basil

Ocimum basilicum

The most popular garden form is sweet basil, *O. basilicum*, although there are many different basils to choose from. Basil is a summer herb in cool and temperate gardens, a warmth lover. In the subtropics and tropics you can grow it year-round. Most forms of basil live for only one growing season, so they are 'annuals'. It's a beautifully aromatic herb in the garden, fragrant to be around as you brush past it.

Growing basics: basil loves sunshine, warmth, fertile, well-drained soil and regular liquid feeds. It grows well from either seed or seedlings. If sowing seeds, sow them shallowly (3mm/0.25in deep); they should germinate in 10–12 days. Space plants about 20cm/8in apart.

Growing in pots: use a good quality potting mix with slow-release fertiliser added, or add a handful of slow-release fertiliser when potting up. A minimum pot size of 20cm/8in top diameter is advisable. Sit the pot on pot feet, to ensure all excess water drains away.

Best time to sow: late spring and early summer.

Picking tips: basil needs to be picked regularly to maintain bushiness. When flower stalks appear, cut these off, plus some foliage, and give plants a liquid feed to encourage more foliage growth.

In the kitchen: basil is at its best fresh, so pick what you need as you go, and use it soon after. *Tip:* basil tends to blacken when cut with a knife, so tear leaves with your hands when adding them to dishes.

Success secrets: basil needs warmth to do well, so in colder areas make sure it is sheltered from cold winds. Regularly cutting it back, and cutting off flowers, will maintain bushiness. Monthly liquid feeds, plus a steady supply of water will keep plants healthy.

Heaven with: tomatoes, and a few torn leaves give a lift to green salads. Use it generously with chillies in Thai stir-fries. It's also the basis of Italian pesto sauce and French pistou soup; it has so many uses it's a must for all herb gardens.

Varieties: sweet basil is the most popular form, growing to 75cm/30in tall; it's what you get when you buy dried basil flakes. Bush basil is a smaller plant 40cm/15in tall, also called Greek basil. Purple basil is readily available, so is ruffled-leafed basil (with either purple or green leaves). Thai basil (*O. horapa*) has a peppery aroma, holy basil (*O. sanctum*) is very aromatic and spicy, lemon basil (*O. citriodorum*) has a lemony tang.

Bruschetta with tomato and basil

Serves 4

1 ciabatta loaf or baguette, cut into 2cm/¾in slices
¼ cup olive oil
2 cloves garlic, roasted and puréed
500g/1lb Roma tomatoes, diced
1 small red onion, finely chopped
¼ cup fresh basil, chopped
1 tablespoon balsamic vinegar
salt and freshly ground black pepper

1 Grill bread slices for 2–3 minutes on each side.

2 Brush with a little olive oil, and spread a thin layer of puréed roasted garlic on each slice.

3 In a bowl, mix together tomatoes, onion, basil, vinegar and 2 tablespoons of the olive oil and season with salt and pepper.

4 Serve grilled bread with tomato mixture on top.

Bay leaf

Laurus nobilis

This is one herb that is well worth adding to your garden, but it's unlike so many other herbs for two good reasons: one is that it's potentially a large tree (up to 11m/36ft tall) and the other is that its leaves are generally valued most as a dried herb, rather than a fresh one. Its botanic name of *Laurus nobilis* refers to its ancient use as a 'laurel crown' worn on the heads of Olympic champions, honoured poets, victorious generals and other notables of Ancient Roman and Greek societies. As bay trees can grow quite tall, in many herb gardens a bay tree is found growing in a large pot, to contain its size.

Growing basics: bay trees grow best in a sunny position in well-drained soil, but will tolerate some shade and are frost-hardy to -7°C/19.5°F. In some climate zones they are prone to attack by scale insects in winter — these can be controlled or, better still, prevented, with regular early-winter spray programs using organic horticultural oil sprays. Fertilise in-ground trees in early spring with well-rotted manure. Bay trees have low to moderate watering needs and cope well with dry periods.

Growing in pots: grow trees in a large, deep pot at least 40–50cm/16–20in across at the top. Sit pots up on pot feet to provide good soil drainage, and feed plants in spring with slow-release fertiliser. Clipping back plants to keep their size down is recommended.

Best time to sow: plant seedlings in spring or autumn.

Picking tips: fresh leaves can be used in cooking, but they will need to be crushed to release their aroma. Most cooks will dry bunches of bay leaves, keep these in sealed jars, and use these in cooking instead. Bay leaves have a strong flavour, so don't add too many (just add as many as the recipe asks for).

In the kitchen: dried leaves are preferred over fresh. Bay leaves are an essential ingredient in soups, stews, casseroles, sauces and marinades.

Heaven with: other herbs (the classic bouquet garni includes thyme, parsley and a bay leaf); all manner of savoury dishes and slow-cooked dishes, but bay also goes well with sweet custards, rice puddings and poached fruits.

Tip: don't eat the bay leaves, just enjoy their flavour.

Chicken jambalaya

Serves 6

1.5kg/3.5lb chicken pieces
2 tablespoons oil
2 onions, chopped
1 clove garlic, chopped
1 green bell pepper/capsicum, chopped
1 celery stalk, chopped
1 cup medium-grain rice
1 cup drained chopped canned tomatoes
2 cups chicken stock
1 bay leaf
pinch of chilli powder
½ teaspoon dried thyme
salt and freshly ground black pepper
1 cup chopped sausage such as salami
¼ cup parsley, chopped

1 Heat oil and fry chicken pieces until golden. Remove from pan and reserve. Add onions, garlic, capsicum and celery and fry over moderate heat until onions are tender. Add rice and toss over heat for about 2 minutes. Add tomatoes and replace reserved chicken in pan. Add stock with bay leaf, chilli powder, thyme, salt and pepper.

2 Bring to boil, cover and reduce heat to simmer. Cook until chicken is tender and liquid is absorbed. Preheat oven to 180°C/350°F. Transfer chicken mixture to shallow ovenproof dish, add sausage and cook in for 10 minutes. Serve garnished with chopped parsley.

Borage

Borago officinalis

If you want to attract bees to your garden, grow some borage, as bees love its pretty blue flowers. This easy-to-grow annual herb, native to southern Europe and western Asia, reaches 60–90cm/2–3ft tall in the garden and will need little attention. It's the star-shaped blue flowers which are mostly used, although the hairy leaves also have a role to play in the kitchen.

Growing basics: borage grows best from seed sown where the plant is to grow – it resents being transplanted. Sow seed in spring in well-drained soil in a sunny spot. Seeds germinate quickly and plants will grow rapidly, and flowering commences in summer and lasts for several weeks. Borage plants are known to self-seed readily in gardens, and so it has potential to become rather weedy if you don't remove seed heads as they form in late summer.

Growing in pots: borage can be grown successfully in a large pot.

Picking tips: simply pick flowers and leaves as needed, during summer.

In the kitchen: the hairy leaves aren't usually left whole; chopping or shredding them is the normal method of preparation. Tender young leaves can be finely shredded and combined with cucumber and sour cream or yoghurt, and the older leaves can be chopped and tossed into a variety of cooked dishes requiring leafy greens. However, it's the sparkling blue flowers of borage which are most popular as a garnish, bringing a mild cucumber flavour to salads. Cake decorators also like to use sugar-coated borage flowers. Borage leaves and flowers don't store well, so try to use them fresh, although they will keep for a day or so, wrapped in paper towel then placed in a plastic bag, kept in the vegetable crisper section of the fridge. Flowers can also be frozen in ice cubes and added to punches and other drinks as a decoration. As well as using borage in salads, it also teams well with herbs such as chervil, dill, mint and rocket (arugula), and it goes well with cream cheese, sour cream and yoghurt.

Borage tea: people have been adding some borage leaves and flowers to tea for many years, and the ancients believed it gave people courage. Alas, *Tyler's Honest Herbal* says: "If you are expecting truly beneficial effects from this plant, try something else. Tests carried out in small animals found borage to be practically inert."

Capers & caperberries

Capparis spp.

There are two products taken from *Capparis* plants which provide a piquant (some say pungent) lemony flavour in cooking: capers, the more strongly flavoured product, and caperberries, with a similar but milder flavour. Capers are the pickled, small, round unopened flower buds of several *Capparis* species, including *C. inermis*, *C. decidua* and *C. spinosa*. Caperberries are the larger, elongated, grape-sized, semi-green fruits of the same plant. The parent plant itself is a many-branched deciduous shrub 2–4m/6–14ft tall, with rounded, fleshy leaves and white flowers in late spring.

Growing basics: native to areas all around the Mediterranean, this shrub can also be grown at home in areas with a similar temperate climate of cool, wet winters and hot, dry summers. It needs well-drained soil and a position in full sun. Plants can be grown from seed sown in spring, or via seedlings raised from cuttings, and once established plants can be long-lived, providing harvests for 20 or more years.

Growing in pots: caper bushes can be grown in large pots.

Harvesting: in commercial production, capers (the unopened flower buds) are picked by hand when they are the right size, then preserved either in salt or vinegar. The caperberries are picked when the fruits are still green, then preserved in vinegar. For home production, caperberries are the easier crop to manage.

In the kitchen: famous sauces such as remoulade and tartare get their flavour bite from chopped capers. Italian pasta sauces such as the quick and pungent puttanesca need capers to work, as does a good tapenade of olives. It's the pungency of capers which makes them so valuable, yet it's also why some tastebuds prefer caperberries, which offer a similar flavour but in a milder form. The best capers are preserved in salt, but vinegar is a common alternative, so to prepare capers or caperberries, first rinse them in water, then either chop or add whole, as the recipe requires. It's best to add them to a dish towards the end of cooking, to preserve the flavour, which deteriorates with longer cooking. Both capers and caperberries go well with many vegetable dishes, in tomato-based pasta sauces, to give a lift to fish and seafood dishes, or add pungency to chicken casseroles just before serving. Capers also team well with other pungent flavours such as garlic, anchovies, mustard and lemon juice, and the addition of olive oil, parsley and oregano can provide the perfect finish.

Pictured left: caperberries

Calamari in garlic and capers

Serves 4

1 carrot, peeled and chopped
1 onion, chopped
½ bunch thyme
8 cloves garlic
juice and zest of 1 lemon
100g/3½oz capers
4 calamari tubes

Marinade
1 teaspoon ground cumin
¾ cup extra virgin olive oil
juice of 2 lemons
1 teaspoon salt
½ teaspoon ground black pepper
8 sprigs lemon thyme

Salad
2 heads radicchio
1 endive
2 teaspoons capers
½ cup flat-leaf parsley, chopped

1 Place carrot, onion, thyme, garlic, lemon juice and zest, capers and 4 cups water in a saucepan, bring to the boil and simmer for 10 minutes.

2 Clean the calamari tubes under running water. Place into the simmering poaching liquid for approximately 2 minutes.

3 Remove the garlic cloves from the poaching liquid and slice. Place the ingredients for the marinade in a bowl, add the sliced garlic and mix together.

4 Remove calamari from the poaching liquid and cut into 5cm-wide strips. Place into the marinade and leave in the refrigerator for 30 minutes.

5 Wash the radicchio and endive, discard the outer leaves, place in a bowl and mix with the capers and parsley.

6 Remove the calamari from the marinade and add to the salad. Use ¼ cup of the marinade as a dressing. Serve immediately.

Caraway

Carum carvi

Archaeologists have discovered caraway seeds in the tombs of Egyptian pharaohs and even in ancient Stone Age sites, so it is one of the world's oldest flavourings. It's still a very popular one, especially in the cuisines of Germany, Holland and Central Europe. It's used extensively in Jewish cooking worldwide and is part of many North African spice blends. The plant itself is a small bi-annual from the Umbelliferae family (also called the Apiaceae family). Though called 'seeds' the caraway we use is actually the small, dried fruits of the plant, which is a summer-growing bi-annual 40–60cm/16–24in high.

Growing basics: caraway is best grown from seed sown in early autumn or spring in a mostly sunny spot with any reasonably well-drained soil. Seeds are harvested at the end of the following summer.

Growing in pots: caraway can be grown successfully in pots.

Harvest tips: cut the seed heads from the plant in late summer then place into a paper bag, then hang this up to collect the seed as they dry and fall into the bag. If growing the plant for its roots, leave to grow on until autumn of the second year before harvesting.

In the kitchen: caraway seeds are popular as a flavouring for breads, crackers and cakes, simply sprinkled on top prior to baking. Caraway, in tandem with juniper, is the classic flavouring for German sauerkraut, and it's also a primary flavouring in Pumpernickel bread. In Hungary it's used in making goulash, and in Morocco it's used to flavour soups, and is a component in various spice blends, including harissa. Try using caraway seeds with rich roasted meats such as pork or goose, sprinkle some caraway seeds into potato dishes for a pleasant new flavour, and team it with apples and sugar when making desserts.

Not caraway: several spices which are not caraway at all have caraway as part of their name. In Turkish cuisine, black caraway is actually nigella, and in Indian cuisine and recipes caraway is sometime listed when the real spice used is cumin.

Blue cheese and onion quiche

Serves 4

370g/13oz prepared shortcrust pastry
2 tablespoons butter
3 onions, thinly sliced
2 cloves garlic, crushed
3 eggs
60g/2oz blue cheese, crumbled
1 cup milk
¾ cup sour cream
freshly ground black pepper
2 teaspoons caraway seeds

1 Roll pastry to fit a 23cm/9in fluted flan tin. Place a sheet of greaseproof paper over pastry, and half-fill with rice. Bake in moderately hot oven for 8 minutes. Remove rice and paper, bake further 10 minutes or until golden brown.

2 Melt butter in a frying pan, add onion and garlic and stir-fry over low heat for about 10 minutes, or until onions are soft and golden brown. Spoon evenly over pastry.

3 Preheat oven to 160°C/315°F. Lightly beat eggs, then add cheese, milk, sour cream, pepper and caraway seeds and gently pour over onions.

4 Bake in oven for 30 minutes or until just set and lightly browned.

Cardamom

Elettaria cardamomum

Usually sold as seed pods (although seeds and powdered seeds are available) cardamom has a pungent, camphor-tinged flavour that is used in many rice dishes, curries, in drinks (including coffee and tea), desserts and sweet treats. The plant itself, *Elletaria cardamomum*, is a strappy-leaf evergreen tropical perennial that belongs to the ginger family, with strap-like leaves 60cm/2ft long, that can form dense clumps 3m/10ft tall. Its flowers appear at the base of clumps, and these are followed by seed pods.

Growing tips: native to southern India, cardamom grows in shady, monsoon forests in tropical and subtropical zones. In temperate zones where it survives as a plant it may have trouble setting seed pods. Generally, it will grow anywhere ginger can be grown. In tropical zones with distinct wet and dry seasons, it dies back in the dry season. Cardamom plants can be grown from seed, and in areas where plants are difficult to obtain this may be the best way to get started.

Harvesting: cardamom is harvested when not quite ripe (ie, pods have not yet split) by hand, a laborious process as the seed pods are close to the ground. The pods are then dried in the sun, or in special hot-air sheds, prior to packaging and sale.

In the kitchen: while it's the seeds and seed pods which are the spice, the leaves of cardamom plants are used to wrap and flavour foods for cooking, including fish, chicken and dessert sweets. Sometimes whole pods, after being partly crushed to expose the seeds, are added to dishes such as curries and rice. Other times the seeds, either crushed or whole, are added. Cardamom is used in both sweet and savoury dishes. It has a very strong flavour, so using it sparingly is recommended. Keep whole cardamom pods in an airtight jar. Ground cardamom loses its flavour more rapidly.

Flavour partners: milk, cheese, yoghurt, pastry, breads, coffee, other spices (in blends), rice, meats (lamb, duck, chicken), fruits, pickles, potatoes.

Green & black: there are two types of cardamom pods sold: green and black. The green pods are considered superior quality. Black cardamom comes from another plant altogether (*Amomum* and *Aframomum*) and has a more camphorous flavour, but it is still a very useful spice, although more pungent, and has its own role in Indian cookery in particular.

Cardamom tea: drinking cardamom flavoured tea or hot milk can aid in digestion, and it is a popular additive to coffee all around the Mediterranean, but particularly in the Middle-East. Cardamom is also part of many Indian chai blends.

Baked spiced pears

Serves 4

juice of 1 lemon
25g/1oz butter
3 tablespoons clear honey
5 cardamom pods, split
2 sticks cinnamon or ½ teaspoon ground cinnamon
½ teaspoon caraway seeds
4 small, firm pears, peeled, halved and cored

1 Preheat the oven to 230°C/450°F. Place the lemon juice, butter, honey, cardamom, cinnamon and caraway seeds in a small saucepan. Stir to combine, then heat gently for 10 minutes to allow the flavours to develop.

2 Place the pears, flat-side down, in an ovenproof dish. Pour the lemon juice mixture over the pears, discarding the cardamom pods and cinnamon sticks, if using. Bake for 20 minutes or until the pears are soft, spooning over the juices halfway through. Serve hot, with any juices spooned over the top.

Note The spices combine with the natural sweetness of the pears to create a great ending to a heavy meal. Serve with low-fat yogurt, cream or a dollop of crème fraîche.

Catmint & catnip

Nepeta faassenii, Nepeta cataria

While these are different plants, they do belong to the same genus and always go together in gardeners' minds because of their close association with our feline friends. Catmint (*Nepeta faassenii*) is a very ornamental garden plant which reaches 45–80cm/18–30in tall in the garden and is loved for its blue-grey foliage and lavender flowers. Catnip (*Nepeta cataria*) is taller, reaching about 1m/3ft when fully grown, produces white flowers, but it's not as ornamental as the pretty flowering catmint. However, it is the plant with the famous reputation for appealing to cats, with its mint-like fragrance.

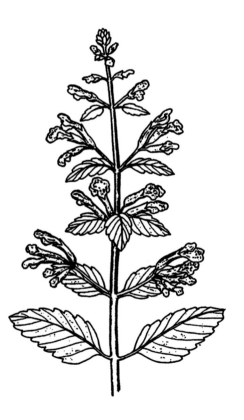

Growing tips: both catmint and catnip like the same growing conditions, doing best in full sun in well-drained soil. Cutting plants back to the ground in late autumn will produce a new flush of foliage and flowers later on, in spring and early summer. Catnip grows easily from seed and will self-seed readily in favourable conditions.

Hit and miss: despite its reputation and name, catnip doesn't work on all cats. Its active ingredient, the chemical nepetalactone, doesn't appeal to young kittens and about a third of adult cats. And for those cats on whom it does have an effect, it's not entirely predictable. While many affected cats seem to be mildly sedated by catnip, others suffer an opposite effect, sending them into a short-lived period of friskiness.

Drying and storing: the best time to cut catnip stems is just before flowering commences. Hang the cut stems inside paper bags to dry, in a dry but airy place. Strip the leaves from the stems and store in an airtight container. A little sprinkling of catnip on puss's favourite toys or sleeping zone will makes its life more fragrant and more interesting.

Did you know? Experiments conducted at major zoos have shown that the kings of the cat world – lions, tigers, pumas and cheetahs – love catnip just as much as our couch-potato domestic cats.

What about catgrass? This useful grass, *Dactylis glomerata*, is a good source of vitamins and minerals for cats and other pets, including dogs, rabbits and guinea pigs. Chewing it can also help cats to remove hairballs. It's very well suited to growing in pots, either on a sunny windowsill or balcony. Reaching just 25cm/10in tall, it can cope with semi-shade.

Pictured left: catmint

Celery leaf

Apium graveolens var. *dulce*

This herb is a leafy variety of the vegetable celery (*Apium graveolens*) that's used widely in many cuisines. Celery leaf plants are closer to the original wild plants and are sometimes sold as wild celery. They have a similar but stronger celery flavour than the more familiar vegetable. Their main advantage over celery is that celery leaf plants are relatively easier to grow in the garden. Asian cooks and gardeners grow and use a lot of celery leaf but it can be used in any cuisine where celery flavour is required. The plant itself grows 40–80cm/16–30in tall, producing long, thin stalks topped with light green celery leaves.

Growing tips: celery leaf can be grown from seed, but germination is slow and can be erratic. Plants are also available as seedlings, and these are an easier way to get started. Sow seed in spring or autumn. Celery leaf grows well in a wide range of climates, from cool temperate through to subtropical but it does best in cooler climates and will need the protection of afternoon shade in warmer climates, It's also more likely to bolt to seed in hot weather. Sow seed in a sunny to partially shaded spot in rich, moist soil, but don't cover seed, as they need light to germinate. Aim to keep the soil lightly moist most of the time. Plants are biennial, so may last more than one year.

Picking tips: harvest whole stalks when they are 20–30cm/8–12in long, with a sharp knife. This will also encourage new stalks to grow.

In the kitchen: you can use celery leaves as a substitute for celery in any dishes requiring celery, but remember it has a stronger flavour, so don't add quite as much. Celery leaves, when chopped, can be tossed into soups, stews and stir-fries. Harvested stems will keep, stored in a plastic bag in the crisper bin in the refrigerator, for two to three days

Water celery: in Asian markets you might also come across 'water celery', *Oenanthe javanica*, an unrelated plant with celery-like leaves, which is popular in Vietnamese cuisine.

Celery seed: another way of adding a celery flavour to your cooking is via celery seed, which has a spicy, slightly bitter flavour that's a cross between nutmeg and citrus.

Ceylon spinach

Basella alba

Gardeners in hot climates sometimes struggle to grow a good supply of leafy salad herbs, as plants such as lettuce and rocket perform poorly in these hot conditions. Ceylon spinach is one plant which can provide lots of nutritious, healthy greens for salads or cooked dishes in hotter climates. Also known as Malabar spinach, Indian spinach and climbing spinach, this is not related to English spinach at all. It's a fast-growing, perennial twining vine of the tropics which produces glossy, green leaves. Two varieties, red-stemmed and green-stemmed, are commonly available to gardeners.

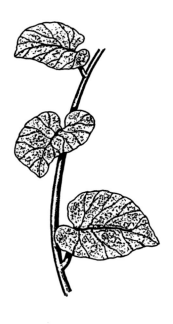

Growing basics: Ceylon spinach thrives in hot climates, or the heat of summer in warm temperate zones, and grows rapidly from seed. In hot climates it will grow as a perennial, producing a steady supply of leaves, but in warm temperate zones it should be grown as an annual over summer, as it won't survive a temperate winter. Make sure to provide a support for this climber to twine up, such as a post, trellis or wire frame mounted on a wall or fence.

Growing in pots: it's best to grow this perennial vine in the ground in hot climates, but in warm temperate areas where it is grown as an annual, it can be grown in large pots, as long as these twining, climbing plants are provided with something to climb up.

Picking tips: simply pick leaves as needed.

In the kitchen: like spinach, Ceylon spinach reduces in bulk to a remarkable degree when cooked, so make sure to harvest a good amount if cooking it in the same manner as spinach. Many cooks prefer to use this purely as a salad herb, uncooked. Ceylon spinach leaves are rich in vitamins and minerals.

Other 'spinaches': Egyptian spinach (*Corchorus olitorius*) is not a climber, but like Ceylon spinach it can be used as both a salad herb and a vegetable, and it too thrives in subtropical and tropical zones. The Japanese leafy green, mibuna (*Brassica rapa* var. *nippisinica*), has similar uses as both a salad herb and vegetable, but it grows best in temperate areas, sown as seed in spring and summer. Mountain spinach, or orach (*Atriplex hortensis*), is a red-leaved plant from the same family as spinach that is a colourful spinach substitute. Warrigal greens (*Tetragonia tetragonioides*) or New Zealand spinach is native to coastal areas of Australasia; but it's best to blanch its thickish, moist leaves briefly in boiling water before using.

Chamomile

Chamaemelum nobile, Matricaria recutita

Several different flowering daisies are commonly known as chamomile, and the two grown most often in herb gardens for making tea and providing herbal remedies are *Chamaemelum nobile* (sometimes called Roman or English chamomile, a low-growing, 10cm/4in tall annual plant) and *Matricaria recutita* (sometimes called German chamomile, a 60cm/2ft tall perennial plant). Both produce white daisy flowers with a yellow centre in summer. Of the two, German chamomile is more fragrant, more potent and more widely grown commercially. Both types of chamomile are native to Europe and North America.

Growing basics: both of these herbal chamomiles can be grown from seed sown in spring, in well-drained soil in a sunny spot in a wide range of climates, but they do best in temperate zones. Many growers raise plants from seed in punnets, then transplant seedlings out later on. German chamomile plants can also be grown from older plants lifted, divided and replanted in spring.

Growing in pots: both types of chamomile can be grown in pots.

Picking tips: pick leaves when young, in spring and early summer, when they have the best flavour. Pick the flowers when fully open in midsummer. The flowers can be used fresh, or sun-dry them then store in an air-tight jar for use later on.

In the kitchen: chamomile has no uses in cooking, apart from making a refreshing cup of tea for a stressed cook (see below).

Chamomile tea: one of the most popular herbal teas, chamomile tea has many claims made in its favour (some claim it's the equivalent of a European ginseng), and it does make a pleasant, refreshing cuppa. There is now solid scientific evidence for some of the claims made about chamomile's benefits, including its ability as a carminative (to aid digestion), an anti-spasmodic (for treating menstrual cramps), as an anti-inflammatory for afflictions of the skin (such as eczema or other rashes), and as an anti-infective agent for a variety of minor ailments. Extracts of chamomile, which are high in its vital oils, are used in making many herbal medicines.

To make a cup of home-made chamomile tea, pour 1 cup boiling water over ¼ cup fresh flowers, or half that amount of dried flowers. Let it stand 5 minutes, then pour through a strainer, add honey to taste.

Chervil

Anthriscus cerefolium

Think 'parsley with a hint of aniseed' and you're getting close to the delicate, pleasant flavour of this biannual herb, *Anthriscus cerefolium*. In fact it also looks like flat-leaf parsley but with smaller leaves. One of the lesser known advantages of chervil is that it does well in semi-shade, while the majority of the popular garden herbs need lots of sunshine. So, for gardeners whose growing spots are less than ideally sunny, chervil is a versatile, pretty and useful herb.

Growing basics: chervil grows best from seed sown into moist, rich soil in a semi-shaded spot. This herb doesn't like to be transplanted, so seedlings are not commonly available, or all that successful. Chervil is grown in spring and summer in cool climates, but in warmer temperate areas it does best from autumn through winter into spring. In areas with hot summers it doesn't do so well.

Growing in pots: chervil is a great choice for growing in pots. Almost any size pot will do, but wide shallow pots give a good supply.

Best time to sow: in cool areas, spring and early summer; in temperate areas any time from autumn through to spring. Chervil is like parsley in that it's a 'biannual' living through two growing seasons, but in temperate zones it's often grown as a long-lived annual.

Picking tips: chervil doesn't keep all that well in the kitchen, so just pick as much as you need each time.

In the kitchen: chervil is one of the herbs in the classic French herb blend called 'fines herbes' (chervil, chives, parsley and tarragon), used in many dishes. Chervil's delicate flavour is appreciated best if you add it, freshly chopped or as a garnish, just prior to serving.

Success secrets: keeping chervil plants away from direct hot sunshine is very important, so too is a steady water supply.

Heaven with: on its own chervil goes well with eggs, and it gives a pleasant lift to all the squash-type vegetables such as squash, zucchini/courgettes and marrows, but it's also very good with most other vegetables, notably asparagus, carrots, beans, fennel, potatoes and peas. Its delicate flavour is very welcome in light soups, salads, with fish and poultry. This is one herb that cooks like to team with other herbs — a blend of tarragon and chervil is popular.

Varieties: there is a curly form of chervil, *Anthriscus crispum*, which is similar in flavour and growing needs as the more common flat-leafed chervil.

Crayfish with green herbs

Serves 4

650g/22oz crayfish or lobster
3 tablespoons extra virgin olive oil
salt and freshly ground black pepper
2 small potatoes, peeled
2 medium tomatoes, diced
¼ avocado, diced
1 small Lebanese cucumber, peeled and diced
1 sprig chervil, chopped
1 sprig tarragon, leaves removed and stalk discarded
30g/1oz baby cos lettuce

Bouquet Garni

3 sprigs parsley
2 large bay leaves
3 sprigs thyme
3 sprigs tarragon

Court Bouillon

2 cups dry white wine
2 carrots, peeled and sliced
2 stalks celery, sliced
1 onion, sliced
1½ teaspoons coarse sea salt
5 black peppercorns

1 Prepare the bouquet garni. Bundle the herbs together and tie firmly with kitchen string.

2 To make the court bouillon, combine the white wine, vegetables, sea salt, peppercorns, the bouquet garni and 4 cups water. Bring to the boil, then immerse the crayfish for 6 minutes. Drain and allow to cool.

3 Remove the meat from the shell, keeping the tail intact. Extract all the meat from the joints and legs. Slice the tail flesh into medallions and finely dice the meat from the legs along with the small end pieces of the tail. Drizzle the tail medallions with 1 tablespoon oil, season with salt and freshly ground black pepper, then lightly grill.

4 Cook the potatoes in boiling water until cooked, about 20 minutes. While still warm, slice the potatoes into small rounds and set aside. Combine the tomato, avocado and cucumber with the herbs and the chopped crayfish, and season to taste.

5 Divide the tomato mixture between 4 serving plates. Place the baby cos on top, then finish with the grilled crayfish medallions and potato slices. Drizzle with the remaining olive oil and serve.

Chickweed

Stellaria media

Many gardeners might be surprised to discover that this common, invasive, difficult-to-control garden weed is not only edible, but also has claimed medicinal benefits. So, rather than tossing handfuls of it into the waste bin, some of it could make its way into your kitchen instead.

Growing basics: chickweed is not a plant that you'd want to introduce into garden beds deliberately, as it is a weed by name and nature, spreading prolifically once established. Bearing small oval-shaped leaves, it's a low-growing plant 15–20cm/6–8in tall that spreads and self-seeds in any moist soil in positions ranging from full sun to shade, in temperate climate zones. Chickweed also bears tiny white star-shaped flowers at any time of year. It's more likely that your garden will already have some chickweed growing, so just harvest and use it, but don't encourage it.

In the kitchen: the fresh leaves, which have a light tang, can be added to salads, tossed into a juicer or blender when making fruit smoothies, or liquidised with vegetables when making health drinks. It can be also included in any dish of mixed, cooked greens.

Medicinal benefits: while various claims are made for the medicinal benefits of chickweed, most notably its ability to relieve itching, to promote healing and relieve constipation, Dr Varro Tyler sums up his opinion of it by saying: "I can think of no good reason to allow space to this worthless weed." It is traditionally applied as a poultice to ease skin diseases, and it is sometimes taken internally to ease problems with the lungs (eg, bronchial asthma) or the stomach and bowels. Alas, the scientific evidence for all these claims is lacking, and the best suggestion Dr Tyler has for it is that it "makes tasty salads or cooked greens". Chickweed is eagerly eaten by chickens, budgies, canaries and most cage or aviary birds.

Chicory

Cichorium intybus

This salad herb comes in many different forms, but the most familiar is green leaves narrow at the base, wider and rounded at the top, with short-lived, blue daisy-type flowers in summer and autumn. A herbaceous perennial native to the Mediterranean, this hardy perennial's leaves usually have a bitter flavour, although the inner leaves are milder tasting.

Growing basics: chicory grows easily from seed in a wide range of soils. It likes a sunny to partly shaded position and reaches 30cm/1ft tall and 25cm/10in wide. Cutting off the flower stems is a good way to encourage more leaf growth.

In the kitchen: younger chicory leaves are the best choice for salads, and if plants are in flower the flowers are edible. Chicory leaves will keep in a plastic bag in the vegie crisper for two to three days. It's a better idea to cook the older leaves, and in Greek cuisine, chicory is cooked either on its own or with other leafy greens, to make the vegetable side dish, horta.

Witlof: this is a form of chicory developed in Belgium as both a vegetable and salad green. It is also called 'Belgian endive', and the name witlof means 'white leaf'. Witlof are created from the regrowth which occurs when all the top growth of the chicory plant is cut away just below ground level. This regrowth is grown in darkness so that the leaves remain pale. The harvested witlof is 10–12cm/4–5in long, a tightly packed barrel of white leaves with pale yellow tips and edges. Picked witlof should be wrapped in plastic, then kept in a brown paper bag, and stored in the dark to prevent greening, which can make the leaves too bitter. Individual witlof leaves make attractive serving 'dishes' for fillings when creating finger food for parties. Whole witlof are often braised in stock and served as a vegetable side dish.

Radicchio: this is Italian type of chicory whose bitter-tasting red leaves are mostly used in salads, but sometimes also in cooked dishes. The inner leaves have the mildest flavour. It grows in sun or partial shade.

Endive: another salad green related to chicory, *Cichorium endivia* also has a slightly bitter taste when added to a salad of mixed greens. Several forms are grown, including frilly-leaved endive. It too grows in sun or partial shade.

Coffee substitute: the roots of chicory have long seen it dried then processed to form a caffeine-free coffee substitute.

Chillies

Capsicum frutescens, C. annuum

Originally from South and Central America, chillies have spread around the world since Europeans discovered the New World in the late 15th century. All chillies are varieties of *Capsicum*, including the most numerous and popular varieties based on either *C. annuum* or *C. frutescens*. All are members of the Solonaceae family of plants, which includes potatoes, tomatoes and eggplants.

Growing tips: chillies are easy-to-grow plants which are treated as fruiting annuals in many climates, although some varieties will grow longer, as perennials. They'll grow in the humid tropics and subtropics year-round, but in temperate and cool-temperate regions they are planted in spring and crops are produced in summer. Plants need plenty of sunshine, fertile soil plus regular watering and feeding when young, but once established reduce feeding to encourage flowering and fruit production. Plants grow readily from seed or seedlings.

Growing in pots: chillies make excellent container plants, and in cooler climates can even be brought indoors to escape frosty weather, provided pots are placed in a warm, sunny spot.

Harvesting: regularly harvesting chillies will encourage the production of more flowers and fruits throughout the growing season.

In the kitchen: handling chillies requires care, especially with the hotter varieties. Many cooks use disposable gloves as a precaution, but as a rule always wash your hands and chopping boards straight after handling chillies. To lessen the heat, remove the inner membranes and seeds. All that said, chillies have countless uses in many cuisines, adding not just their famous fiery heat but also a lot of flavour, depending on the variety used. There are also many very mild chillies whose heat is minimal, used in cooking for their flavour.

Chilli products: as well as fresh chillies used in cooking, dried chillies (as flakes or a powder) are a major spice. Whole dried chillies are a key ingredient in Mexican and other cuisines. Chilli sauces (such as the famous Tabasco) and chilli oils are also plentiful, and preserved chilli products such as the Sambal Oelek of Indonesia, and chilli jams, are now used worldwide.

Cooling the heat: capsaicin is soluble in oil or fat – not in water – so to cool the burning of chilli take full-cream milk or yoghurt to dissolve the capsaicin. Or, if you're desperate, some oil (bread dipped in oil is more palatable than just drinking oil). Drinking water, beer or wine won't do much to soothe the burning.

Heat scales: famous for their heat, chillies are rated according to the Scoville heat scale. As an example, a hot chilli such as the Cayenne rates at 30,000 units on this scale (and a mildish Jalapeno chilli, 5000) but the current world-record-holder for chilli heat, the Trinidad Scorpion Butch T chilli, rates at 1,463,700 on this same scale. These are so hot that even to hold one in your hand requires the wearing of rubber gloves, to avoid burns.

Chilli crab

Serves 4

2 medium (or 1 large) crab
3 tablespoons vegetable oil
1 tablespoon lemon juice
salt

Sauce
2–3 red chillies, seeded and chopped
1 onion, peeled and chopped
2 cloves garlic, peeled and chopped
2 teaspoons grated fresh ginger
2 tablespoons vegetable oil
2 ripe tomatoes, skinned, seeded and chopped,
   or 2 teaspoons tomato paste
1 teaspoon sugar
1 tablespoon light soy sauce
3 tablespoons water

1 Clean the crabs thoroughly, then cut each body into 2 or 4 pieces. Chop or crack the claws into 2 or 3 pieces if they are large. Heat the oil in a frying pan, add the crab pieces and fry for 5 minutes, stirring constantly. Add the lemon juice and salt to taste, remove from the heat and keep hot.

2 To make the sauce, put the chillies, onion, garlic and ginger in a blender and work to a smooth paste. Heat the oil in a wok or a deep frying pan. Add the spice paste and fry for 1 minute, stirring constantly. Add the tomatoes, sugar and soy sauce and stir-fry for 2 minutes, then stir in the water. Add salt if necessary and simmer for a further 1 minute. Add the crab and stir to coat each piece in the sauce and cook the crab through, only a minute or two. Serve hot.

Note If using live crabs, the best way to handle them is to wrap them in paper and put in the freezer long enough to numb them. Then pierce and cut through eyes and shell, or with a heavy cleaver cut quickly in two.

Chives & garlic chives

Allium schoenoprasum, A. tuberosum

Both these members of the onion family are valuable kitchen herbs which are well suited to growing in pots. They're similar but different and worth growing in a herb garden, but as growing them is so similar we have teamed them together here. Chives (*Allium schoenoprasum*) is a clump-forming perennial herb with grass-like, hollow leaves, about 30cm/1ft high, with a pleasant oniony flavour. Originally from North American and Northern Europe, it produces mauve to pink round flowers in late spring and summer. Garlic chives (*A. tuberosum*) is slightly bigger, its flat leaves are 50cm/18in tall, and it has a stronger, slightly garlicky flavour. Native to central and northern Asia, it produces white star-shaped flowers in summer.

Growing tips: both plants can be grown in the ground or in pots, and both start equally well from seeds or seedlings. Full sunshine, rich, well-drained soil and monthly liquid feeds will keep plants growing well in their growing season. As plants form clumps they will need to be lifted, divided and replanted every second year. The cooler the climate zone, the more likely it is that chives might die down in winter but they will resume growth in spring. Garlic chives often will grow on during winter in cooler zones.

In pots: both chives and garlic chives are very well suited to pots. However, potted plants will need to be divided and repotted every year, during winter, as the clumps often spread to fill the pots rapidly and, after that happens, clumps can wilt due to root competition and lack of moisture and nutrients.

In the kitchen: chives combine well with chicken, eggs, fish, potato, cucumber, celery, salads, soups, mayonnaise and vinaigrettes. They are an excellent ingredient in tartare sauce with fish. Chives are usually prepared by chopping or snipping handfuls (kitchen scissors make this easy) into small pieces. Chives have a delicate flavour, so they are best added to dishes just before serving – don't overcook them. Garlic wchives, with their stronger flavour, are added earlier on in cooking many dishes. They go well with chicken, fish, pork, eggs, salads and soups, but as garlic chives are a key ingredient in Chinese cookery you will find them used with many other ingredients, from beef to tofu and many vegetables. Chive flower buds are sold as a vegetable in Asian food stores. You can also use garlic chives to flavour vinegars. To store leftover garlic chives or chives, place them in a plastic bag in the refrigerator, where they will last two to three days more.

Asparagus, ricotta and herb frittata

Serves 4

500g/1lb fresh asparagus, trimmed to 15cm/6in
    lengths
12 medium eggs
2 small cloves garlic, crushed
1 cup mixed herbs, including basil,
    chives and parsley, chopped
salt and freshly ground black pepper
60g/2oz butter
100g/3½oz ricotta
squeeze of lemon juice
olive oil or truffle oil, to drizzle
parmesan, to serve
fresh chives, to garnish

1 Preheat the grill to high. Place the asparagus in a grill pan and grill for 10 minutes or until charred and tender, turning once. Keep warm.

2 Meanwhile, whisk together the eggs, garlic, herbs and seasoning. Melt 30g/1oz of the butter in an ovenproof frying pan until it starts to foam, then immediately pour in a quarter of the egg mixture and cook for 1–2 minutes, stirring occasionally, until almost set.

3 Place under the preheated grill for 3–4 minutes, until the egg is cooked through and the top of the frittata is set, then transfer to a plate. Keep warm while you make the 3 remaining frittatas, adding more butter when necessary.

4 Arrange a quarter of the asparagus and a quarter of the ricotta over each frittata, squeeze over the lemon juice, season and drizzle with oil. Top with shavings of parmesan and garnish with fresh chives.

Cinnamon

Cinnamomum verum

With its warm, sweet and fragrant scent, this versatile spice is, like pepper, one so highly valued since ancient times that wars were fought to secure its supply. Originally from Sri Lanka, *Cinnamomum verum* (syn. *C. zeylanicum*) is a tree 8–17m/26–55ft high that is now grown in plantations in many tropical countries, including Sri Lanka, southern India and Burma. It's the bark of the cinnamon tree which produces the spice, sold as woody 'sticks' or in powdered form.

Growing tips: this is a largish tropical tree not well suited to gardens outside the tropics and subtropics. Plantation-grown cinnamon trees are much smaller, regularly cut to the ground every few years and harvested to encourage the growth of new shoots. The tree's young leaves are red and mature to dark glossy, green. The flowers are small and pale yellow with a foetid smell. Purple berries follow the flowers. It prefers a sunny or slightly shaded position and well-drained soil.

Harvesting: in plantations, three-year-old trees are coppiced (cut back to just above the ground) when growth is 2–3m/6–10ft tall, for easy harvesting. New shoots develop for three more years, harvested, and the cycle continues. It's the inner bark of the tree which is harvested, processed and dried to form the cinnamon sticks (also called quills). These long, tightly rolled quills are the best quality. However, nothing is wasted in processing and broken pieces are used in making ground cinnamon.

In the kitchen: cinnamon is one of the spices in savoury Chinese 'five spice mix'. Its sweetness lends itself to all manner of cakes and biscuits. Used whole or powdered, it goes beautifully with apples, pears, quinces and stone fruit, and in Greek cuisine a rice pudding wouldn't be right without some cinnamon on top. In Italy cinnamon is dusted over cappuccino coffee, and in Morocco whole cinnamon sticks are part of many different tagines.

Cinnamon substitutes: cassia bark from *Cinnamomum cassia* is often sold misleadingly as cinnamon, and has a common name of false cinnamon. Its bark is dark brown and thick, while real cinnamon bark is thin, light brown and in quill form multi-layered. Cassia also has a coarser, more bitter flavour.

Cinnamon tea: just a pinch of powdered cinnamon can add an extra layer of warmth to any cup or pot of tea. Lemon juice goes well with cinnamon tea, as does honey. If you are in the tropics, where cinnamon leaves are available, these can be used to make tea, too.

Apple and cinnamon cupcakes

Makes 12

½ apple, peeled and chopped into small pieces
juice of 1 lemon
1 tablespoon cinnamon powder
3 eggs
½ cup butter, softened
1 cup superfine/caster sugar
½ cup milk
1½ cups self-raising flour, sifted

Topping
1½ cups confectioners'/icing sugar
½ cup butter, softened
1 tablespoon cinnamon sugar

1 Preheat the oven to 160°C/320°F. Line a 12-cupcake pan with cupcake papers. In a small bowl, coat the apple pieces with lemon juice and sprinkle with cinnamon. In a medium-sized bowl, lightly beat the eggs, add butter and sugar, then mix until light and fluffy.

2 Add milk and flour, and stir to combine. Beat with an electric mixer for 2 minutes, until light and creamy. Add spiced apple and stir through mixture.

3 Divide the mixture evenly between the cake papers. Bake for 18–20 minutes until risen and firm to touch. Allow to cool for a few minutes and then transfer to a wire rack. Allow to cool fully before icing.

Topping
Combine half the icing sugar and butter, mix with a wooden spoon, add remaining icing sugar and butter and beat with the spoon until light and fluffy. Spoon topping onto cupcakes and sprinkle cinnamon sugar on top.

Citrus flavours

Citrus spp.

In many cuisines the delights of fresh citrus used to be available only during the harvest seasons, so people devised ways of preserving citrus fruits so their flavour could be enjoyed year-round, and each culture has developed its own distinctive approaches.

Growing basics: all citrus need well-drained soil, regular watering and day-long sunshine. There are many varieties, so climates ranging from tropical through to cool temperate zones can grow citrus suited to their conditions. Generally, warm temperate and subtropical zones can grow the greatest variety of citrus.

Growing in pots: citrus can be grown in large pots, minimum diameter of 40cm/16in, measured across the top.

In the kitchen: in North African cookery, lemons are cut into sections and preserved in jars packed with salt and lemon juice. It's the thick rind of the lemon which is most used, added to flavour tagines of fish or chicken in particular. In the Persian Gulf states (Iran, Iraq) limes are first boiled whole then sun-dried to preserve them (leaving the limes black or brown once dried). Known as black limes, these are then added to soups and stews containing vegetables, legumes, seafood or poultry, either as whole dried limes, or as crushed powder. Citrus peel is dried in many countries, using citrus particular to each region (eg, a small citron called yuzu in Japan, tangerine or orange in China, lemon in North Africa). The dried peel is sometimes added straight to dishes to impart a citrus flavour, but in some cases (such as with dried tangerine and orange in Chinese cookery) it is soaked prior to being used. Candied (sugared) lemon and orange peel has many uses in making cakes, desserts and pastries in Western cookery generally.

Preserved lemons: making your own preserved lemons is something you can try at home. Wash 4 lemons then cut each into quarters, from the top almost to the bottom, but leaving the base of each lemon intact. Open out each lemon and pack with sea salt. Place the salted lemons into a sterilised jar, pack them in tightly, then sprinkle in more salt. Pour in enough lemon juice to cover. Seal the jar and leave in a dark cupboard for four weeks. To use, rinse each lemon under cold water, pat dry, them cut rind from flesh and discard flesh and pith. Chop rind and add to Moroccan tagines.

Citrus meringue pie

Serves 6

Shortcrust Pastry
2½ cups plain flour
1 teaspoon superfine/caster sugar
250g/8oz unsalted butter, chilled and cut into small
   squares

Citrus Filling
5 egg yolks
1½ cups sweetened condensed milk
juice of ½ lemon
juice of ½ lime
juice of ¼ orange
1 egg white

Meringue Topping
5 egg whites
¾ cup caster sugar

1 Preheat oven to 200°C/400°F. To make pastry, place flour, sugar and butter in a food processor and process until mixture resembles fine breadcrumbs. With machine running, slowly add iced water until a firm dough forms. Turn dough onto a lightly floured surface and knead until smooth. Wrap dough in cling wrap and refrigerate for 30 minutes.

2 Roll out dough to fit a 20cm/8in pie dish. Line pastry case with non-stick baking paper, half-fill with uncooked rice and bake for 10–15 minutes. Remove rice and paper, and cook pastry case for 5–10 minutes longer or until pastry is golden. Set aside to cool. Reduce oven temperature to 150°C/300°F.

3 To make filling, place egg yolks, condensed milk, lemon juice, lime juice and orange juice in a bowl and mix to combine. Place egg white in a small bowl and beat until stiff peaks form. Fold egg white into egg yolk mixture and spoon into pastry case. Bake for 10–15 minutes.

4 To make topping, place egg whites in a large bowl and beat until frothy. Gradually add sugar, beating well after each addition. Continue beating until stiff peaks form and the mixture is glossy. Cover filling with meringue. Bake for 10 minutes or until topping is golden.

Cloves

Syzygium aromaticum

One old name for the Indonesian archipelago was 'The Spice Islands', and one of the most prized of all the spices from this equatorial region was cloves, the highly aromatic dried flower buds of the tropical tree, *Syzygium aromaticum*, which is native to the Molucca Islands. Though this is one spice plant which is very hard to grow in most gardens, the spice itself is an essential inclusion in any spice cabinet. It's a key flavour in cuisines ranging from China, to South-East Asia and South Asia through to the Middle-East and into Europe and the Americas.

Growing tips: this equatorial tree needs year-round heat, humidity and rainfall in order to grow and flower successfully, so only gardeners in the humid tropics should try growing this tree, which can reach 20m/66ft tall in the wild, but much smaller in the garden.

Harvesting: the flower buds are picked well before they begin to open into flowers, then are sun-dried until they turn blackish-brown. In tropical plantations, flowers are harvested twice a year (times vary depending on the monsoon season's timing).

In the kitchen: the essential oil within cloves can evaporate quickly, so always store whole cloves in an airtight container, kept in a dark cupboard. Powdered cloves will lose their flavour more rapidly, so always buy small amounts and use up rapidly. The culinary uses of cloves are many, and vary with the cuisine, but in all cases, moderation is the best policy with this powerfully flavoured spice. It's one of the ingredients of Chinese five spice powder, Indian garam masala, and French quatres épices, and it's used in many other spice blends worldwide. In fact, with that strong, individual flavour cloves are more likely to be used as part of a spice blend, rather than a flavouring on its own. In Europe, cloves are a pickling spice, they often team with onions to flavour stocks and sauces. Along with spices such as cardamom and cinnamon, cloves spice many rice dishes in the Middle East and India. And sweet dishes based on fruits, notably apples, include a touch of cloves for added fragrance and flavour.

Clove tea: this is such a pungent spice that you will need just a tiny pinch of powdered cloves to transform a cup or pot of tea. One whole clove can be added to the pot, if preferred. Cloves' famous soothing effect on aching teeth is one reason many drink it, but it's equally useful for people with muscular aches and pains.

Stout-glazed ham

Serves 20–30

7½kg/16lb cooked leg of ham
40 cloves
2 cups stout beer
170g/6oz soft brown sugar
2 tablespoons mustard
1 teaspoon ground ginger
2 teaspoons ground cardamom

1 Preheat oven to 160°C/320°F. Remove the skin from the ham leaving a portion of skin around the bone. Score the ham with diagonal lines in both directions and put a clove in the centre of each section. Place ham fat-side up in a roasting dish and pour over 1¾ cups of the stout. Bake for 3 hours, basting occasionally with stout. Remove ham from oven and baste thoroughly.

2 Increase oven temperature to 200°C/400°F. Combine sugar, mustard, ginger, cardamom and enough remaining stout to make a paste. Spread mixture over ham and bake for 35 minutes or until well glazed.

Comfrey

Symphytum officinale

A popular inclusion in any medicinal herb garden, comfrey was one of the original herbal wonder plants which was valued for its ability to heal wounds, and the good news is that science agrees, it does work. One of its other, ancient, common names was 'knitbone'. However, comfrey is not a plant for the kitchen garden, as ingesting it is potentially harmful to health. The plant itself is a hardy perennial about 1m/3ft tall, producing flowers in spring and summer, which can be white, purple or pink, although purple is the colour most well-known.

Growing basics: there are many varieties of comfrey grown in gardens, but *Symphytum officinale* is the one with the best medicinal properties, so make sure that is what you're growing. Several other, ornamental forms of comfrey are smaller and prettier plants with better flower displays. Seeds aren't very reliable as a way of getting started (as germination is slow and erratic), so most growers plant root cuttings or a division (with roots) taken from another plant. Plant comfrey in a sunny or semi-shaded spot in rich, well-drained soil, in early spring. In winter plants die down; at this time cut them back hard and add the cut-down parts of the plant to the compost heap, as it will help speed the composting process.

Growing in pots: comfrey needs to be grown in large pots, as it has a large taproot which needs a good depth of soil.

Picking tips: pick leaves and flowers as needed in preparations; the roots are valued in herbal medicine as well.

In the kitchen: comfrey has no safe uses in the kitchen, as ingesting it is now known to be potentially harmful to health. Some older herbal books do recommend making a tea to drink, but this is dangerous.

Comfrey uses: a popular herbal remedy for many centuries, 'comfrey tea' is not to be drunk, so don't take it internally. It is used instead as a poultice, applied externally to the skin, to help heal wounds. *Tyler's Honest Herbal* says research shows that its reputation as a healing herb does have a basis in science, as it is high in allantoin, an agent that promotes cell growth. And research also backs up the warning not to drink the tea, as it contains an alkaloid hazardous to health, which has potential carcinogenic properties

Coriander seed & leaf

Coriandrum sativum

This annual herb growing 60cm/2ft tall is *Coriandrum sativum*, which is called coriander in some countries, and cilantro or Chinese parsley in others. It's a versatile plant, equally valued as a fresh herb, of which all parts – stems, roots and leaves – can be used. Coriander can also be used as a whole or ground spice made from the dried seeds crushed in a mortar and pestle.

Growing basics: it grows in either partial shade or full sun, but well-drained, fertile soils are essential, as are monthly liquid feeds. This is a fast-growing herb which is often harvested commercially as whole plants when they reach 40cm/18in tall. In the garden in hot weather it can 'bolt to seed' rapidly, where its foliage changes from wide leaves to spindly ones, and flowers soon form, followed by seed heads. In temperate zones it grows better, and a bit slower, in autumn, winter and spring. In hotter zones it needs to been grown quickly and harvested often.

Growing in pots: coriander grows well in pots, monthly liquid feeds and regular picking will keep plants bushy.

Best time to sow: coriander grows well from seed or seedlings. While it can be grown year-round in temperate and tropical zones, it's a better garden herb away from the hot summer months.

Picking tips: pulling up whole plants is a good way to use coriander, as all parts of the plant are usable in cooking. Otherwise, keep picking leaves regularly to maintain bushiness.

In the kitchen: coriander is a key ingredient in cuisines ranging from Mexico to Thailand, Vietnam, India and the Middle-East. The roots are often used in South-East Asian curry pastes, the chopped stems cook down easily, and the fresh leaves are a popular garnish for many dishes. Coriander has a strong aroma and flavour (which not everyone loves) so using it in moderation as a garnish is recommended.

Not coriander: Vietnamese coriander is also called Vietnamese mint, but it's neither coriander nor mint, it's *Periscaria odorata*. It has a very hot and peppery flavour quite unlike coriander.

Coriander the spice: the dried seeds of the coriander plant are one of the world's most popular spices, a key flavour in cuisines ranging from North, Central and South America to the Mediterranean, the Middle-East, the Indian subcontinent and East Asia. The two main types of coriander seed sold are the spherical Moroccan type and the oval-shaped Indian type. Prior to being ground into the spice, the seeds are dry-roasted. As a whole spice, coriander is often used in making pickles. Coriander is found in many spice blends, including Indian curry powders.

Beef pho

Serves 6

225g/8oz thick steak in one piece
1 packet rice noodles
2 tablespoons fish sauce
455g/15oz flat, thick, dried noodles
½ cup of bean sprouts, washed
1 brown onion, thinly sliced
3 spring onions, finely chopped
½ cup fresh coriander, torn into sprigs
½ cup Vietnamese mint leaves, chopped
1 small red chilli, seeded and sliced into rings
2 limes, cut into wedges

Stock
3 litres/6.5 pints water
1kg/36oz shin beef bones
340g/12oz gravy beef
1 large brown onion, unpeeled and halved
3 medium pieces fresh ginger, unpeeled and sliced
pinch of salt
1 cinnamon stick
6 whole cloves
6 peppercorns
6 coriander seeds
4 whole star anise
2 carrots, unpeeled and cut into chunks

1 To make stock, pour the water into a large pot, add the shin bones and gravy beef and bring to the boil. Skim off foaming scum from surface. Turn heat to medium-low, partly cover and simmer for 2 hours, skimming often. Add remaining stock ingredients. Simmer for another 90 minutes and remove from heat.

2 Drain through a fine sieve, reserving stock. Discard bones, carrots, onion and spices. When cool, skim fat from stock. Cut the gravy beef finely across the grain. Slice steak to paper thin slices and set aside.

3 Soak the rice noodles in warm water for about 20 minutes until soft. Drain and set aside.

4 Return stock pot to boil. Add the fish sauce then reduce heat to very low. Fill a separate large pot three-quarters full of water and bring to the boil. Add the dried noodles and bean sprouts. Continue boiling until noodles are tender but not mushy. Bean sprouts should retain some crispness.

5 Pour boiling stock into six serving bowls, add drained noodles then top equally with gravy beef slices, raw onion rings, spring onions, and raw steak slices, and garnish with coriander and mint leaves.

Note Diners may help themselves to chilli rings and lime wedges. This recipe is also good with chicken which takes less time to cook.

Cornflowers

Centaurea cyanus

This charming flowering annual is a wonderful addition to any herb or salad garden, mostly for its pretty blue flowers in spring and summer, but they do have the handy bonus of providing edible flowers to decorate a green garden salad. While herbs themselves can produce an array of pretty flowers at various times of year, the sight of cornflowers rising above the greenery of a herb garden during spring and summer is well worth enjoying. The common cornflowers grown in gardens are annuals ranging from 30–90cm/1–3ft tall, with grey-green, lance-shaped leaves. While blue is the most common flower colour for the thistle-like blooms, you can also get cornflowers with white, pink, yellow, mauve and maroon blooms.

Growing basics: cornflowers are easily grown from seed and produce their flowers during spring and summer. Plant seeds in full sun, in rich, well-drained soil in spring. Fertilise regularly with a soluble plant food.

Growing in pots: cornflowers can be grown successfully in pots.

Picking tips: pick flowers for salads as needed. You can also pick cornflowers as cut flowers for vases indoors. Pick the stems in the early morning, scald the base of the stem in hot water, then plunge into clean water.

In the kitchen: the cornflower's main use in the kitchen is as a pretty edible garnish for summer garden salads. Cornflowers are often also dried before being added to potpourris.

Cornflower tea: dried cornflower petals are included in some herbal tea blends, so you can try doing this at home by combining some dried petals with green leaf tea. Cornflower petals are part of the Lady Grey blend of tea sold commercially by Twinings.

Medicinal uses: while traditional herbal medicine practitioners use cornflower petals externally to treat minor wounds, ease mouth ulcers and conjunctivitis, the scientific evidence for its efficacy is lacking. Cornflowers also have many uses in the making of cosmetics.

Cress

Nasturtium officinale

Watercress, the salad herb, is *Nasturtium officinale*, but there are several other edible plants called 'cress', including the flowering plant called nasturtium or Indian cress, which is *Tropaeolum majus*. Garden cress is from yet another genus, *Lepidium sativum*, and land cress is *Barbarea verna*. Despite their differences, they're all plants whose rounded leaves have a peppery flavour, hence the common name of cress for each.

Growing basics: watercress is the main plant grown for use in the kitchen (but see page 172 for our tips on growing and using nasturtium, *Tropaeolum majus*). As its name implies this fast-growing aquatic plant grows best in a sunny spot in flowing water, and it is also grown hydroponically. Though flowing water is ideal for watercress, it can be grown in water-filled tubs, changing the water regularly. Many home-growers prefer to plant it into compost-enriched potting mix in pots, and this needs to be always moist. One way to get started is to buy watercress plants from the markets which still have fine, white roots attached. These will continue growing on in water, back at home. Even watercress plants without roots can be placed in a jar of water, and those which sprout roots can then be grown on. Land cress is a hardy biennial which prefers moist ground in semi-shade to shade, and isn't fussy about soil types, but it doesn't like frosts. It's a better choice for gardens than trying to grow watercress. Garden cress is a taller-growing pant (up to 45cm/18in), likes cold and dry growing conditions and is very hardy.

Growing in pots: all the cresses can be grown in pots.

In the kitchen: cress is a salad herb with a peppery flavour, so the main thing is not to add too much to a salad – its role is to be a lively part of a mixed leaf salad. A few leaves are often included in sandwiches to add interest. Cress is also added to a wide variety of soups, often in tandem with cream, yoghurt or milk. Cress gives vegetable soups a lift, and it is often turned into a sauce to serve with fish. It combines well with fennel, parsley and sorrel, and complements cucumber, oranges and other salad greens. In Chinese cookery cress is often tossed into stir-fries, and is sometimes treated as a stir-fried green side dish on its own.

Watercress and apple salad

Serves 4–6

1 large bunch watercress
2 green apples
1 tablespoon lemon juice
4 tablespoons sunflower or light olive oil
3 tablespoons cider vinegar
1 teaspoon prepared mustard
salt, pepper to taste

1 Wash the watercress well, shake dry then pluck the sprigs from the stems and wrap in a clean towel, refrigerate to crisp for 1 hour.

2 Cut the apple into four leaving skin on. Cut out the core and slice thinly. Place in a bowl and sprinkle with lemon juice.

3 Toss the watercress and apple together in the serving bowl. Whisk the oil, vinegar, mustard and seasonings together, pour over the salad and toss gently.

Cumin

Cuminum cyminum

This spice comes from the seeds of a 30-50cm tall annual plant, *Cuminum cyminum*, whose foliage looks like fennel's. Originally from Egypt it is now grown in many countries in regions where the summers are dryish and not humid. Cumin seeds (technically speaking, a fruit) look like caraway and fennel seeds, are small and thin, about 5mm/0.25in long and 2mm/0.1in across, yellowy-brownish in colour, with ridges running along their length.

Growing tips: it's easy to grow cumin from bought cumin seed sown in spring in moistened soil, once any danger of frosts has passed. Plants grow best in full sun in fertile, free-draining soil. Flowering (in pink or white) in summer is followed by the seed heads, these taking a few weeks to mature. Cumin prefers a hot, dry summer, and hates humidity, so warm, Mediterranean-style climates suit it best.

Harvesting: keeping an eye on the seed heads forming is needed to judge the best time to harvest. These can be dried in the sun, if weather permits, or in paper bags hung up in a dry, airy place.

In the kitchen: both whole cumin seed and powdered cumin seed are used in the kitchen. It's best to make only as much powdered cumin as you need each time, first dry-roasting seeds until lightly fragrant prior to crushing. Cumin is a vital ingredient in curries and many other south Asian dishes, curry pastes and powders, but it's also a key ingredient in North African cooking, the Middle-East, South and Central America and Mediterranean cuisines.

Goes with: other spices, such as allspice, cardamom, cloves, coriander, fenugreek, paprika, turmeric, saffron, and chilli. On its own it goes very well with vegetables, such as beans, cabbage, potatoes, eggplant and squash family members, but it is used in so many dishes that it is a classic 'mixer' of the spice cupboard.

Black cumin: this is a source of confusion. There is a darker-coloured type of cumin seed called black cumin (called kala jeera in India), but there is another product called black cumin which is not cumin at all: this is *Nigella sativa* (called kalonji in India) which is a small black seed which resembles onion seeds and is also often labelled as black onion seed. Another black cumin, which looks more like cumin and caraway, is from the plant, *Bunium persicum*.

Cumin tea: made from the seeds steeped in hot water, this is taken for medicinal purposes more than for its earthy, slightly bitter flavour.

Tikka skewers

Serves 4

500g/1lb chicken tenderloins
oil for cooking
1 lemon, cut into wedges

Spicy Yoghurt Marinade
1 small onion, chopped
3 cloves garlic, crushed
1cm/0.5in piece ginger, chopped
1 tablespoon ground cumin
1 tablespoon garam masala
2 cardamom pods, crushed
1 teaspoon ground turmeric
1 teaspoon chilli powder
1 teaspoon ground coriander
1 tablespoon tomato purée
1¼ cups natural yoghurt

Cucumber Raita
1 cucumber, finely chopped
¼ cup fresh mint, chopped
1 cup natural yoghurt

1 Pierce tenderloins several times with a fork and place in a shallow ceramic or glass dish.

2 To make marinade, place onion, garlic, ginger, cumin, garam masala, cardamom, turmeric, chilli powder, coriander and tomato purée in a food processor or blender and process until smooth. Add yoghurt and mix to combine. Spoon marinade over chicken, toss to combine, cover and marinate in the refrigerator for 3 hours.

3 Preheat barbecue to a medium heat. Drain chicken and thread onto lightly oiled skewers. Place skewers on lightly oiled barbecue grill and cook, turning several times, for 5–6 minutes or until cooked.

4 To make raita, place cucumber, mint and yoghurt in a bowl and mix to combine. Serve skewers with lemon wedges and raita.

Curry leaf

Murraya koenigii

A few different plants share the common name of 'curry leaf' but the one with many uses in Asian cuisines is a small tree, *Murraya koenigii*. Native to elevated parts of India, Sri Lanka and Burma, this grows to 3–5m/10–16ft in the garden and produces long strands of leaflets which are, botanically, just the one leaf. These leaves (also called meeta neem, or kari patta) are best used fresh in cookery, but dried curry leaves are available.

Growing tips: this small tree does best in tropical and subtropical climates, but it can grow in warm, frost-free temperate zones. It copes with full sun or partial shade. After flowering it produces red berries which turn black, but these are not used in cookery and it's the fresh green leaves which are harvested for the kitchen. As curry trees come from the same family as citrus, similar growing methods, including feeding and watering, apply. Plants are partially deciduous, and so may die back in the dry season in the tropics, and in winter in temperate zones.

Growing in pots: it does very well in a pot. A minimum pot size of 40cm/16in across, measured at the top, is recommended, so too are slow-release fertilisers.

In the kitchen: curry leaves are used either at the beginning of cooking, or at the end. Used at the start, they are tossed into hot oil to flavour the oil prior to adding the other ingredients. Used at the end of cooking, they are chopped and either stirred into the dish in the final moments or scattered over the top as a garnish.

Tip: when recipes call for '10 curry leaves' they mean 10 leaflets, removed from the stem. Curry leaves go well with fish, lamb, lentils, rice and most vegetables, and they combine well with many other spices in pastes (and dried, in powders).

Dried curry leaves: these are often sold and have an inferior flavour to fresh leaves. Use more generously, to compensate for the weak flavour.

Curry leaf tea: this has a rather mild flavour, so be generous in your use of curry leaves when experimenting with your first brew. Packaged, dried-leaf curry leaf tea is available; its claimed benefits include a reduction in nausea.

The wrong curry leaf: the so-called 'curry bush' is a low-growing, silver-leafed plant (*Helichrysum italicum*) which gets its misleading common name from the spicy fragrance of its leaves, but it's not useful in the kitchen.

Bombay hot lentils

Serves 4

200g/7oz mung dhal (small yellow lentils),
   cleaned and soaked
½ teaspoon ground turmeric
25mm/1in piece fresh ginger, finely chopped
1 tablespoon vegetable oil
salt and freshly ground black pepper
1 tablespoon tamarind pulp
1 tablespoon brown sugar
½ bunch fresh coriander, leaves removed
   and chopped
3 tablespoons flaked coconut
2 teaspoons garam masala

Whole Spice Mixture
90g/3oz ghee or butter
1 teaspoon cumin seeds
1 teaspoon black mustard seeds
¼ teaspoon fenugreek seeds
2 tablespoons chopped curry leaves
3 fresh red or green chillies, finely chopped
50mm/2in piece fresh ginger, finely chopped
salt

1 Place 2 cups water in a large saucepan and bring to the boil. Stir in lentils, turmeric, ginger, oil, salt and pepper to taste and cook over a low heat, stirring occasionally for 30–45 minutes or until lentils are very soft. Remove pan from heat and mash lentil mixture.

2 Place tamarind in a small bowl, pour over 1 cup hot water and set aside to soak for 20 minutes. Drain liquid from tamarind mixture, then push tamarind pulp through a fine sieve and set aside. Reserve juice for another use.

3 For spice mixture, heat ghee or butter in a separate large saucepan, add cumin seeds, mustard seeds, fenugreek seeds, curry leaves, chillies, ginger and salt to taste and cook, stirring for 1 minute.

4 Add lentil mixture and 4 cups water to spice mixture and bring to the boil. Stir tamarind pulp and brown sugar into lentil mixture and cook, stirring occasionally for 5 minutes longer.

5 Stir in fresh coriander, coconut and garam masala and cook for 2 minutes longer.

Dandelion

Taraxacum officinale

One of the most widespread garden weeds of the world, dandelions need little introduction to gardeners, but some people may be surprised to discover that this weed has some handy culinary uses, and a few applications in medicine as well. Its old common name of 'piss-a-beds' refers to its diuretic effects, which are well-known and also scientifically proven. However, the long list of other medical benefits claimed for dandelion have little scientific backing. Its botanical species name of 'officinale' (common amongst herbs and spices) signifies that this is the 'official' species used by apothecaries. This low-growing (10–20cm/4–8in tall) weed with broad, tooth-edged leaves sends up bright yellow, 5cm/2in diameter flowers from spring through to autumn.

Growing basics: most gardeners don't so much grow dandelions as fail to stop them growing, as this is a common weed in gardens. Often found growing in lawns, dandelions also pop up wherever their fluffy, floaty seed balls manage to land and establish a spot in gardens.

Growing in pots: dandelion will grow in pots, sometimes even when not asked to do so. As it has a long taproot, pots need to be fairly deep.

Picking tips: the young leaves of dandelions have the best flavour; older leaves tend to be bitter. Remember, however, to harvest dandelion leaves only from lawns and other garden areas which have not been treated with any chemical sprays. Always wash the leaves thoroughly prior to adding them to salads.

In the kitchen: the main use for dandelion is as a summer and autumn salad herb, not on its own, but as part of a salad of mixed garden greens. As well as eating the leaves, the roots of dandelions are also edible. Dandelion flowers are also used in making dandelion wine, an acquired taste; and dandelion roots are roasted and processed to produce another acquired taste, a coffee substitute drink.

Medicinal benefits: while many claims are made for the benefits of dandelion wine and coffee, and medications made from dandelion leaves, it seems the only good evidence to date does confirm that it does have a mild diuretic effect, and a laxative effect as well.

Dill

Anethum graveolens

Anethum graveolens is an annual herb that is called dill weed in some countries. It's grown for its delicate, feathery light green leaves which sit atop tallish stems about 90cm/3ft high. These have a lemon and anise flavour that is a classic companion for seafood, but its flavour is valued in many other cuisines, including those of South-East Asian countries. This is a fairly quick-growing herb which is best treated as a short-term crop which needs regular harvesting and replanting. There is another type of dill called Indian dill (sometimes referred to as *A. graveolens sowa*) which is grown for its seed, a popular ingredient in curry powders and pastes.

Growing basics: dill grows best in full sun but can cope with some shade. Space plants 25–30cm/10–12in apart, and grow them from seed sown directly where it is to grow. Apply a liquid feed monthly and keep well watered in hot weather. When flowers appear, pinch them out, to prolong the production of the leaves for the kitchen. That said, dill is a relatively short-lived herb, and successive plantings of new seed is the best way to maintain a steady supply.

Growing in pots: also grow plants from seed, use a slow-release fertiliser, and maintain a steady water supply at all times.

Best time to sow: spring and early summer.

Picking tips: pick stems as required, as dill doesn't keep for long in the kitchen. If you have an excess of dill, try freezing whole stems in plastic bags to preserve them, rather than trying to dry them.

In the kitchen: use dill fresh on the day you pick it. It chops very easily.

Success secrets: grow dill crops from seed, as it doesn't like being transplanted as seedlings.

Heaven with: dill is the classic herb to use with fish and seafood (it's the basis of the famous Scandinavian salmon dish, gravad lax). It's used extensively in Northern European cuisines with vegetables such as cucumbers, potatoes, cabbage and cauliflower, and Greek cooks couldn't do without it, either, especially in slow-cooked mixed vegetable dishes. South-East Asian cuisines also use dill in soups, seafood dishes and herb blends. Try it with any combination of vegetables; its strong flavour will survive long cooking as well.

Beneficial herb: dill is a beneficial plant to have in the garden as it attracts ladybirds, hoverflies and lacewings which help to control various garden insect pests.

Bitki with dill sauce

Serves 4

750g/24oz minced beef
2 slices stale white bread, crust removed
¼ cup milk
1 medium onion, finely grated
1 teaspoon salt
freshly ground black pepper, to taste
1 tablespoon finely chopped fresh dill
1 egg
½ cup flour for coating
oil for cooking

Dill Sauce
2 tablespoons butter
2 tablespoons flour
1½ cups milk
2 tablespoons lemon juice
2 tablespoons chopped fresh dill
1 egg yolk
salt, pepper to taste

1 In a large bowl place the bread slices and milk to soak. On fine side of grater, grate the onion straight into the bowl to also catch the juice. Add salt, pepper and dill. With a fork, mash the bread and combine all the ingredients.

2 Add the mince in stages, incorporating the bread mixture and knead with hand for a minute making a finer grain mince. Cover and refrigerate for at least 30 minutes.

3 With wet hands shape into 6 patties. Place flour on a sheet of kitchen paper. Heat enough oil to shallow fry the patties. Dip each pattie in flour, shake off excess and fry for 6 minutes each side over moderately high heat. Move to a heated plate, keep hot. Serve hot with the dill sauce and vegetable accompaniments.

4 To make the dill sauce, heat butter in a small saucepan, add flour and stir until it bubbles slightly.

5 Remove from heat, gradually stir in the milk stirring well between each addition. Return to heat, add lemon juice and dill and stir continuously until sauce thickens and boils. Remove from heat, season to taste with salt and pepper and stir in the egg yolk. Stir over the heat for a few seconds without allowing it to boil. Serve hot.

Echinacea

Echinacea purpurea

Also well-known as the cone flower, this attractive perennial member of the daisy family sends up a 1m/3ft tall flower stem topped with a purple-pink bloom whose petals hang down from a high-domed centre. It's a native of North America, and *Echinacea purpurea* is the most commonly grown form in gardens, but *E. angustifolia* is the original wild species. Many echinacea cultivars, with different flower colours and plant sizes, are now available.

Growing basics: plants are usually grown from divisions of existing clumps planted in autumn and winter, although plants also can be started from seed sown in spring. Echinacea needs full sun and well-drained soil and grows best in cool temperate climates, but it can also be grown in warmer areas. Flowering begins in summer and continues into autumn, then plants die down for winter and reshoot in spring.

Growing in pots: echinacea can be grown in pots.

In the kitchen: echinacea's only use in the kitchen is to make a cup of tea.

Medicinal benefits: indigenous North American natives discovered the medicinal benefits of echinacea centuries ago, and they passed this knowledge on to European settlers. Now, an extraordinary number of claims are made for the health benefits of echinacea, and some of them are backed by scientific research. Echinacea has been proven to prevent infections, heal wounds and stimulate the immune system.

It's useful in preventing the common cold and sore throats which result from colds. It's also beneficial in treating infections of the respiratory tract and the urinary tract. However, Dr Varro Tyler, in *Tyler's Honest Herbal*, points out that the quality of echinacea products sold varies widely, and that the method of administering it (ie, as injections, as drinks, in tablet form, etc) affects its usefulness. He advises using the best quality products available.

Echinacea tea: pour 1 cup boiling water over ¼ cup of fresh echinacea leaves, flowers or root, let it steep for 5 minutes, then strain and pour. In winter, when fresh echinacea isn't available, you can use dried leaves, flowers or root to make tea, but halve the amount of dried product when making a brew. Don't use this tea continuously; two to three cups per day is the maximum, and only use it for up to 10 days in succession.

Echinacea spray: brew up some echinacea tea, let it cool, then use this as a healing spray on wounds.

Fennel

Foeniculum vulgare

This plant is so versatile that it's grown as a herb, a spice and a vegetable, all renowned for their aniseedy flavour. It is also so hardy that it is a common roadside weed in many areas. All types are originally from the Mediterranean, but in modern gardens one type of fennel (*Foeniculum vulgare* 'Dulce', or the bronze-coloured *F.* 'Rubrum' and *F.* 'Purpureum') produces the feathery foliage which makes the herb and provides the seeds used as spice. Another type (*F. vulgare* var. *azoricum*) called a Florence fennel (or finocchio in Italy), produces a tender swollen white bulb at its base, used as a vegetable. The herb/spice form of fennel bears yellow flowers in summer, which are followed by the (brown or green) seeds, which are harvested in autumn.

Growing tips: fennel resents being transplanted, so all types are best grown from seed, sown where you want plants to grow. The herb/spice fennel is a perennial which can grow up to 2.5m/8ft tall and can last in the ground for many years, while the vegetable form of fennel is smaller (about 60cm/2ft tall) and it's harvested about three to four months after seed is sown. Sow seeds 1cm/0.5in deep in fertile, well-drained soil in a sunny spot (although plants can cope with some shade), and once growing well thin out plants so they are spaced 40–50cm/16–20in apart.

Pots: these are not really ideal, as fennel grows better in the ground, but if you want to try it, grow a single plant in a 30–40cm/12–16in diameter pot that's at least 30cm/1ft deep.

In the kitchen: the herb fennel goes well with fish, egg dishes and vegetables, and can be used as a substitute for dill. The vegetable form of fennel is delicious, very finely sliced, in salads, where its aniseedy flavour gives a lift. When baked it loses that aniseedy flavour and takes on a pleasing sweetness. The spice called fennel is most often used as a seed, and it's found in many classic spice blends, from Indian garam masala and panch phoron, through to Chinese five-spice powder and many other blends. Fennel seeds have a bittersweet aftertaste which is lessened, and made sweeter, by dry-roasting. Fennel's aniseedy flavour goes well with vegetables such as beans, cabbage, cucumber, lentils, potatoes and tomatoes, and it also teams nicely with duck, pork, chicken and seafood.

Fennel tea: slimmers swear by fennel tea to help them lose weight. The tea is usually made from the fresh leaves, not the spicy seeds. Scientific studies show it is an aid to digestion which can alleviate problems with gas.

Fenugreek

Trigonella foenum-graecum

Originally from southern Europe, fenugreek (*Trigonella foenum-graecum*) is a summer annual 70cm/28in tall. It's grown for both its fresh leaves, which are used in cooking, and its harvest of seeds, which are an important spice in Middle-Eastern and Indian cookery, but also in many other cuisines, particularly throughout Asia.

Growing tips: depending on their freshness you can probably grow some fenugreek from bought seed. Simply sow the seeds in spring where you want them to grow, cover lightly with soil, water in well and they should germinate. These are annual plants, lasting just the one growing season (spring and summer). If using the fresh leaves harvest what you need when they are young. If wanting the seeds, allow the plants to go through the full life cycle of flowering (it has yellow flowers) and setting seed, then collect the seed in autumn.

Growing in pots: fenugreek can be grown in pots. As with all potted plants, they will need more regular watering than plants grown in the ground; apart from that growing is the same as for in-ground plants.

Harvesting tips: the seeds are produced inside long, pea-like pods which turn brownish and begin to split from one end when ripe, usually in autumn. Pick the pods and spread the seeds to dry fully before storing in airtight jars.

In the kitchen: fenugreek seeds are more commonly used than the fresh leaves. Seeds are amber in colour, cuboid (chunky) about 3–4mm/0.25in across, and are used either whole or ground. Fenugreek is one of the five spices in the key Indian spice blend called panch phoron (meaning five seeds) which combines whole seeds of fenugreek, cumin, fennel, black cumin and black mustard. Fenugreek is said to reduce the 'fishiness' of fish dishes, but on its own it is bitter-tasting, so it is often used by frying it first in oil to reduce its bitterness and flavour the oil. Fenugreek the spice goes very well with most vegetables and combines well with spices such as cardamom, cloves, cumin, coriander, fennel and turmeric. Fresh leaves, which have a grassy flavour, should be used soon after purchase or harvest, as they only last a few days. Toss them into salads, add to potato and other vegetable dishes.

Tea potential: fenugreek tea, made using the seeds or the leaves, is believed to be an aid for breastfeeding mothers, for diabetes sufferers and those with digestive problems. Honey improves its flavour.

Feverfew

Tanacetum parthenium

This medicinal herb, formerly *Chrysanthemum parthenium*, has long been valued for its beneficial effect on moods, and research now shows that it can be useful in treating migraine headaches. The plant itself is a hardy perennial 60–120cm/2–4ft tall that's covered by small white daisy flowers with yellow centres through summer. It grows wild in Europe and North America and is a pretty, easy-care inclusion in many herb gardens. Various cultivars of feverfew are available, including some with double flowers and others with decorative golden leaves.

Growing basics: feverfew loves a very sunny spot in the garden in well-drained soil. You can grow it from its very fine seed sown in spring (which is fiddly to handle, so mix seed in with fine sand and sprinkle that mix over a prepared garden bed). You can also grow plants from cuttings taken in summer, or by a division (with roots) taken from an existing clump in autumn. Once established, this is an easy-care plant with few pest or disease problems. It self-seeds very easily, so it is potentially an invasive weed. Plants should be cut back when flowering ends in late summer or early autumn.

Growing in pots: feverfew is easy to grow in pots. In cold climates growers bring their potted plants into shelter for the winter.

Picking tips: it is the leaves of feverfew which have the medicinal benefits, so it's best to pick these in spring, before the plant flowers, then hang these up to dry to use as a medicine (store dried leaves in an airtight jar in a cupboard).

In the kitchen: feverfew is edible but it is so bitter that it is rarely used.

Medicinal benefits: recent studies have shown that feverfew can ease the pain of arthritis, and can also reduce the number of migraine headaches, which offers flow-on benefits such as improved sleep. To take feverfew, you only need to consume two to three leaves a day. These are very bitter, so adding in a sweeter herb such as mint is recommended, as is taking feverfew and mint together in a small sandwich of bread. Taking more than two to three leaves a day is not recommended – it can lead to mouth ulcers. *Tyler's Honest Herbal* says that studies also show that eating the plant's leaves seems to be more effective than taking extracts from the plant in tablet form.

Galangal

Alpinia galanga

Commonly called Thai ginger, galangal is a member of the ginger family. Galangal (*Alpinia galanga*, *A. officinarium*) is a perennial plant with long, narrow aromatic leaves forming a clump 1–2m/3–6ft tall. Like other culinary gingers, galangal is grown for its rhizomes (thick roots) which are used in many South Asian and South-East Asian curries, curry pastes, stir-fries and other dishes. It can be an attractive, tropical-look garden plant with its long, green leaves.

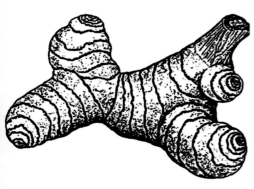

Growing tips: doing best in tropical or subtropical zones, galangal is easy to grow at home from rhizomes planted 50–100mm/2–4in deep and 60cm/2ft apart, with the buds facing up. In temperate areas choose a warm, sheltered frost-free spot and plant in spring, once the weather warms. Fresh rhizomes bought in a shop are fine for planting – just make sure it has a bud (raised portion) on it, from which new shoots will emerge. As with other gingers, galangal likes a semi-shaded spot, in rich, well-drained soil. Regular watering and feeding will ensure better growth. In cooler temperate areas, plants will die down in winter, reshooting next spring.

In pots: you can grow galangal in a large large pot (50cm/8in across at the top).

Harvesting: dig up rhizomes as needed. If you can, leave some of the fresh new shoots and the youngest, pink-tinged rhizomes in the ground, and take the larger, older rhizomes found at the base of the older leaves.

In the kitchen: galangal rhizomes are knobby and pale orangey-brown in colour with distinct dark rings. After peeling, rhizomes are usually chopped, grated or sliced before being added to dishes or to make pastes. Its flavour is both aromatic and spicy, similar to but distinctly different from ginger, with a lemony tang. It's a key ingredient in curry pastes in Thailand, Cambodia and other South-East Asian cuisines, flavouring many different curries, stews, satays, sambals, soups and sauces. It goes especially well with vegetables, chicken, seafood, chilli, coconut, fish sauce and garlic. To store leftover rhizome, wrap loosely in aluminium foil and keep in the vegie crisper section of your fridge for a few weeks.

Greater and lesser: there are two types of galangal – lesser (*A. officinarum*) a smaller grower, and greater (*A. galanga*) the larger plant.

Galangal tea: galangal can also be used to flavour tea. It has a lemony tang. Start with just a little, sliced or chopped, to flavour a pot of green tea.

Chicken and coconut soup

Serves 6

3 cups coconut milk
500g/1lb chicken breast fillets, cut into
   1cm/0.5in-thick strips
4cm/2in piece fresh galangal or ginger, sliced
2 stalks lemon grass, cut into 4cm/2in pieces
1 fresh coriander root, bruised
4 kaffir lime leaves, shredded
3 fresh red chillies, deseeded and chopped
2 tablespoons fish sauce
2 tablespoons lemon juice
¼ cup fresh coriander leaves

1 Place coconut milk and 2 cups water in a saucepan and bring to the boil over a medium heat. Add chicken, galangal or ginger, lemon grass, coriander root and lime leaves and simmer for 6 minutes.

2 Stir in chillies, fish sauce and lemon juice. To serve, ladle into bowls and scatter with coriander leaves.

Note This popular Thai soup is known as Tom Kha Gai. When dining in the traditional Thai manner, soups are not served as a separate course but are eaten with the other dishes and rice. Don't eat the lemon grass, just enjoy its flavour.

Garlic

Allium sativum

A member of the onion family, garlic (*Allium sativum*) is a mainstay of cuisines all around the world. Many varieties of this pungent bulb are available, varying in size, colour and flavour. As it grows, each garlic clove planted forms a new bulb (containing up to a dozen cloves) and sends up a tall (30–60cm/1–2ft) stalk with long, upright leaves topped in summer with round white, blue or pink flowers.

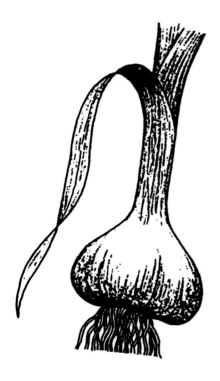

Growing tips: garlic is better suited to areas with cool, frosty winters, but it can be grown in warmer areas as well. Generally, in cool climates grow 'hardneck' garlic and in warmer areas choose 'softneck' varieties. Garlic needs a position in full sun plus light, fertile, well-drained soil to grow well. Garlic cloves are planted from autumn through winter and into early spring. Plant cloves 5cm/2in deep, with the pointed end facing upwards (so it's just below soil level when covered with soil), spaced 15–20cm/6–8in apart. Liquid-feed monthly after the first shoots appear, or apply a side-dressing of manure beside the line of plants.

In pots? Not really, but you can try if you like. Pots need to be kept cool on warm days, to keep soil temperatures down, so place your pot of garlic inside another, larger pot, to help keep it cool.

Harvesting: garlic is ready to harvest when the foliage begins to yellow and die back (in early, mid or late summer, depending on where it's grown). Pull up whole plants and hang them up in a dry, airy place until fully dry (this can take several days). If you don't want to wait that long, you can eat garlic when young. Called green garlic (or garlic scrapes in the US), it is eaten leaves and all, added to soups, stews and stir-fries.

In the kitchen: once dried, garlic has a long storage life in a dry, dark spot in the kitchen. Its uses are infinite, as it goes with most herbs, spices and savoury dishes. Garlic also roasts very well on its own, turning into a sweet, mild creamy-textured paste. It's a key part of many curry pastes and other sauces in cuisines worldwide.

Medicinal benefits: though not a popular tea, garlic is one of the world's oldest and most popular herbal remedies. Its proven health benefits include treatment of high blood pressure, heart disease and gastro-intestinal problems. Its unproven health benefits are many and indeed almost endless in their variety, but the active chemical in garlic, alliin, when crushed, takes on antibiotic properties.

Aromatic lemon roast chicken

Serves 4

1 bulb garlic, cut in half crosswise

2 lemons, cut into thin wedges

3 cardamom pods

1 teaspoon cumin seeds

4 cloves

1¼kg/2lb 13oz chicken

2 tablespoons olive oil

salt and black pepper

¾ cup chicken stock

½ tablespoon plain flour

1 Preheat the oven to 180°C/350°F. Place half the garlic bulb and half the lemon wedges in a roasting tin. Lightly crush the cardamom, cumin and cloves with a mortar and pestle and add to the tin. Tuck a few of the remaining lemon wedges under the breast skin of the chicken and the rest inside the cavity along with the remaining garlic half.

2 Place the chicken in the tin, breast-side down, brush with oil and season. Add 2 tablespoons of stock, cover with foil and cook for 1 hour. Turn chicken over, baste, then roast for a further half hour or until cooked – the juices should run clear when the thickest point of the thigh is pierced with a skewer.

3 Remove the chicken from the tin. Strain the juices, skim off any excess fat, return juices to the tin and stir in the flour. Cook gently for 1 minute, stirring, then add the remaining stock and simmer for 2 minutes, stirring. Serve the chicken with the gravy spooned over the top.

Note Infused with spices and garlic, and slow-roasted on a bed of lemon, this chicken is an exotic alternative to the usual roast. And its juices make wonderful gravy.

Ginger

Zingiber officinale

Used in cuisines worldwide, ginger is one spice which is equally valuable in both its fresh and dried, powdered forms, although the flavours and uses of each are very different. The ginger plant itself is grown commercially in tropical and subtropical climate zones, but it's so easy to grow that it will grow in frost-free temperate climates. There are many ornamental, flowering forms of ginger which are not used in cookery, but the culinary variety is *Zingiber officinale*, grown for its tuberous rhizomes (roots).

Growing tips: ginger plants reach 1.5m/5ft tall in gardens. In the tropics and subtropics it grows best during wet summers then dies down in the winter dry season. In temperate zones, plant it in spring in a warm, sheltered spot to get good summer growth, then harvest in autumn. Plants prefer shelter from the hottest midday sun, and a position which gets morning sun, with well-drained soil, is ideal. Plants are grown from pieces of rhizome kept back from harvest for replanting.

Harvesting: when it reaches two years old, the rhizome is dug up for harvest. Roots can be harvested earlier than this, to produce milder-flavoured green ginger.

In the kitchen: fresh ginger is an essential ingredient in many curry pastes, often teamed with garlic and chillies, but its culinary uses are many, including the making of fruit-based desserts. After peeling, fresh ginger can be chopped, grated, sliced or crushed before being used in cookery; it's also crushed and squeezed to extract ginger juice. Some cuisines make a distinction between using 'young' smooth-skinned, tender ginger (with a mild flavour) and 'old' rougher-skinned ginger (with a stronger flavour).

Dried or ground ginger: this is an important spice in its own right, made from dried and processed fresh ginger, but it doesn't have the same flavour as fresh ginger. Used in European cookery to make cakes and desserts, it's also one of the essential spices of Middle-Eastern and North African cuisines.

Pickled ginger: known as gari in Japan, pickled ginger is a common side dish in Japanese and Korean cookery. It retains much of the bite of fresh ginger, but with its own texture.

Ginger tea: this is where fresh ginger and ground ginger can both be used, depending on the flavour you want. Many claims are made for the benefits of ginger, but there is solid scientific evidence for its ability to relieve motion sickness for travellers.

Beef keema

Serves 4

3 tablespoons vegetable oil
2 onions, sliced
1 clove garlic, crushed
1cm/0.5in piece fresh ginger, finely grated
500g/1lb lean beef mince
¼ cup fresh coriander, chopped
1 fresh red chilli, chopped
¼ cup natural yoghurt
2 cups brown rice
4 cups beef stock
2 whole cloves
1 cinnamon stick

1 Heat oil in a frying pan over a medium heat. Add onions, garlic and ginger and cook, stirring, for 3–4 minutes or until onions are golden and tender. Add beef and cook, stirring, for 5 minutes or until beef is well browned.

2 Stir coriander, chilli and yoghurt into beef mixture and cook for 1 minute. Remove pan from heat.

3 Place rice, stock, cloves and cinnamon stick in a large saucepan and bring to the boil over a medium heat. Reduce heat to simmering, cover and simmer for 45 minutes. Remove pan from heat and stand, covered, for 5 minutes.

4 Lightly fork onion and beef mixture through rice and heat over a low heat, stirring, for 4–5 minutes, until keema is heated through.

Ginkgo

Ginkgo biloba

The ginkgo tree, also called the maidenhair tree because of the distinctive shape of its foliage, which resembles that of the maidenhair fern, is a remarkable survivor from 200 million years ago that some like to call a 'living fossil'. Native to China, *Ginkgo biloba* is a very long-lived, large (25m/80ft tall and 10m/33ft wide) deciduous tree whose green leaves turn a buttercup yellow in autumn. Greenish catkins occur on the male tree, and the female bears paired pale yellow, edible fruit whose aroma bothers some people, but not others. These trees are very hardy once established, and found in parks and gardens worldwide, and in some cities they are grown as street trees. Due to the unloved aroma of the female tree's seeds, the street and park trees are usually male ginkgo trees.

Growing basics: the ginkgo tree needs full sun and does best in cool temperate zones, although its autumn foliage colour show in mild temperate zones is still very appealing. The main issue with growing this tree is its great size when mature. It needs a large garden, where it makes a superb shade tree. However, in order to have crops of edible seeds, you will need two trees (one male, one female) further putting demands on garden space.

Growing in pots: no, they're so big they are unsuitable for growing in pots.

Picking tips: the outer, fleshy part of the seeds, harvested from female plants, don't smell that great, say some, but once removed the seeds inside – called ginkgo nuts – are edible.

In the kitchen: ginkgo nuts have a mild taste, and many people purely eat them for their medicinal benefits, rather than their flavour.

Gingko seeds are also available as a canned, ready-to-eat product.

Medicinal benefits: various preparations containing ginkgo are found in health shops worldwide, with its adherents valuing their benefits on the lungs, to alleviate high blood pressure, improve memory and ease urinary problems. Extracts made from ginkgo leaves are used in making herbal medicines, and the scientific backing for its effectiveness is impressive, with studies showing it is useful in improving blood flow with many applications, such as memory difficulties (particularly in the elderly and those suffering from Alzheimer's), plus dizziness, tinnitus and headaches.

Ginseng

Panax ginseng

This mainstay of traditional Chinese medicine is often referred to as a herb, even though it's the root of the plant which is most used. In Chinese medicine it is used as a restorative and revitaliser. As with any drug, it is important to use it under medical supervision, and so growing it for self-medication is not recommended. Ginseng can have negative side-effects particularly for pregnant women, children or people with heart disease. Its botanical name of *Panax* comes from the Greek word 'panax' which means to heal. There are two species grown commercially: Asian ginseng (*Panax pseudoginseng*) and American ginseng (*P. quinquefolius*), although there are 11 species of ginseng known. Though native to China, East Asia and North America, ginseng is now grown in many countries.

Growing tips: ginseng grows best in cool, highland areas outside the tropics, and forms a 30–45cm/12–18in tall perennial with toothed oval leaflets. It produces small yellow or pink flowers in summer, which are followed by red berries. It needs a rich, well-drained, soil in a shady spot. Generally it's grown from seed in early summer. In winter it dies back, but plants are extremely cold-tolerant and reshoot in spring. Plants aren't ready for harvesting (in autumn) until they are five to seven years old. Snails and slugs are the main pest problem.

Harvesting: the roots are harvested in autumn, and plants are long-lived (up to 100 years or more). The roots are a bit like a two-pronged parsnip and this forked shape looks like a man's legs: the Chinese character for 'ren', part of the plant's name, ren shen, looks like a man's legs.

Medicinal uses: this medicinal root is used fresh, sliced or chopped, or dried, usually as a powder. Dried ginseng leaves are also used in traditional medicine. There are many claims and disputes about the medicinal uses of ginseng, and caution is advised.

Ginseng tea: fresh spring and summer flowers can be used in teas. Powdered ginseng root is also used in making teas, and ginseng flavoured teas are widely available, often in combination with other herbs. There is solid scientific evidence that ginseng helps to reduce stress and promote general well-being; however one problem remains that the quality of ginseng products varies widely, and not all products sold as 'ginseng' actually contain ginseng.

Horseradish

Armoracia rusticana

Grown mostly for its hot, pungent roots, horseradish (*Armoracia rusticana*) is a member of the Brassica family, along with wasabi, mustard, cabbages and broccoli. The plant itself, originally a native of South-Eastern Europe and western Asia, is lush and leafy to 1–1.5m/3–5ft tall, but it's the deep, beige coloured taproot which is harvested for eating mostly as a condiment to accompany other foods.

Growing tips: horseradish grows well in most climates, except the wet, humid tropics and arid zones. It not only grows well in cool climates, it's said that exposure to intense cold is needed to produce the best flavour. Deep, fertile, well-drained, sandy loam soil is needed to grow it well, and plants are usually grown from a section of fresh root, planted 3–5cm/1.5–2in deep. Potted plants are often available in nurseries in spring. A position in full sun is best. Please note that plants grow so easily from even small bits of root that it can become invasive and weedy.

In pots: deep pots are needed to grow horseradish, but otherwise they can be successful grown this way (and this is a good way to control its weediness). Regular watering and good soil drainage are essential.

Harvest: you can harvest young roots growing from the side of the plant, as needed. Otherwise, dig up the whole plant in autumn. Younger roots are preferred, as older larger roots can have a woody central core which cannot be grated for use.

In the kitchen: when used and grated fresh, horseradish discolours fairly quickly and loses its pungency rapidly as well, so it is often mixed with vinegar or lemon juice to preserve its colour and flavour. Its flavour is intense and hot, a blast to the sinuses, but not long-lasting. Its hotness doesn't survive cooking, either. It's a traditional accompaniment to meats such as roasted beef, but stirred into sour cream or yoghurt, plus a dash of vinegar, it makes an appealing condiment (called horseradish cream) to go with fish or chicken. If grown at home, horseradish leaves can be used in dishes, much like spinach or mustard leaves, bringing a peppery flavour to dishes such as soups and stir-fries. A variety of horseradish flavoured sauces and condiments are made for various cuisines, often teamed with cream and, sometimes, other fruits or vegetables.

Wasabi substitute: much of the commercially sold 'wasabi' paste is actually horseradish paste with a green colouring. Horseradish and wasabi are closely related and their flavours are similar, if different.

Juniper

Juniperus communis

Most famous in the West as the source of the name for the popular spirit alcohol, gin, juniper berries are the fruit of a pine, *Juniperus communis*. This pine (in several different forms) grows naturally across the northern hemisphere. Juniper berries are 1cm/0.5in in diameter and change from green when young and unripe to purplish-black when ripe. The ripe berries have a pleasant, resinous aroma and are found only on female juniper plants (although male plants are needed for pollination to produce the 'berries' which are, botanically speaking, tiny, flesh-covered pine cones). One male plant is enough to produce berries on several females.

Growing tips: the ideal climate for growing these attractive small evergreen pine trees (or shrubs) is one with a cold, moist winter. Winter-long snow on the ground is not a problem.

In the kitchen: these resinous flavoured berries have found fame as the key flavour in the distilled spirit, gin (whose name come from the Dutch word for the berry, jenever). However they have many uses in Scandinavian and Central European cuisines in sauces and marinades, especially when cooking game such as rabbit, hare, game fowl and venison. In addition to its uses with game meats, it also combines well with cabbage (in German sauerkraut, for example) and apples, and herbs such as bay leaves, caraway, garlic, marjoram, rosemary and thyme. The fresh berries have the best flavour, but in many areas all that's available are dried berries, which have an inferior flavour. Cooks usually lightly crush fresh berries before using them, to release the flavour.

Medicinal uses: the Ancient Greeks and Egyptians both used juniper as a medicine, rather than as a spice/flavouring. Its diuretic properties have long been valued (and have been proven by modern researchers), but it is no longer recommended for those with kidney disorders (for which it was once traditionally prescribed).

Berry careful: while some other juniper species also produce edible berries, some species' berries are toxic, so great caution is advised if you are not certain which species of *Juniperus* you find berries on.

Korean mint

Agastache rugosa

This plant (*Agastache rugosa*) and its cousin, anise hyssop or licorice mint (*A. foeniculum*), are both worth growing in herb gardens not only for their aromatic leaves but also for their pretty heads of purple summer flowers. As their names name imply, anise hyssop has an aniseed flavour and Korean mint has a peppermint flavour, although it is not related to mint (*Mentha* spp). Korean mint is native to Korea and Eastern Asia generally, and is a short-lived perennial herb 1–1.2m/3–4ft tall spreading 60cm/2ft wide. Its aromatic, oval-shaped, pointy-ended, mid-green leaves have pronounced serrations down the sides, plus white, hairy undersides. In summer it sends up numerous 15cm/6in long flower spikes filled with small purple flowers.

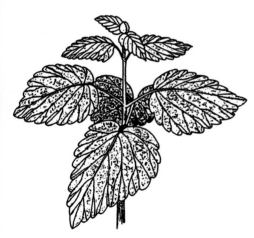

Growing basics: Korean mint does best in full sun in well-drained, fertile soil. It can be grown from seed or cuttings, and herb specialists sell seedlings ready for planting in spring. Being native to Korea, these plants are frost-hardy, but they should be cut back after flowering ends, in autumn. Plants should also be lifted, divided and replanted every two to three years, in spring. Many growers also take cuttings in late summer or early spring, to maintain their supply of plants, which tend to be short-lived.

Growing in pots: Korean mint can be grown in medium to large pots outdoors.

Picking tips: simply pick fresh, young leaves as needed in the kitchen. They are at their aromatic best in spring, just before flowering starts.

In the kitchen: think 'mint' when using it. This plant's leaves, stems and flowers are used, although it's the leaves which are most commonly added to salads, marinades and sauces, and to make cups of tea (see below). Korean mint's flavour goes very well with summer fruits, and teams easily with many vegetables, including beans, root vegetables, tomatoes and zucchinis, and meats such as lamb and pork.

Korean mint tea: just as many different mints make a wonderfully refreshing cup of tea, Korean mint, with its peppermint tang, does the same. Either make a cup of Korean mint tea on its own, ¼ cup of fresh leaves to 1 cup boiling water, and let it steep 5 minutes before pouring. Or add some Korean mint to flavour a pot of green tea. Add honey or sugar to taste. Korean mint is said to relieve symptoms of indigestion, and is used in Chinese medicine to treat respiratory disorders and head colds.

Lavender, English

Lavandula angustifolia

While there are many different forms of lavender to add colour and fragrance to any garden, there is really only one lavender which is a valuable addition to the culinary herb garden, and that's English lavender, *Lavandula angustifolia*. The other popular garden lavenders, variously called French lavender (*L. dentata*), and Spanish lavender and Italian lavender (*L. stoechas*) have a much less appealing flavour with a distinct camphor aftertaste. So, our recommendation is to only grow English lavender in your culinary herb garden, and that's the plant we are describing below. English lavenders bloom from about mid-spring to midsummer; their flowers can be used in cooking and, commercially, they are processed to make lavender oil.

Growing basics: English lavender needs full sunshine and well-drained soil (in fact sandy or gravelly soils are ideal); they enjoy a good, steady supply of water from autumn through to spring but they will do best in areas where summers are relatively dry. They don't like summer humidity and plants may not thrive in these climate zones (however other lavenders, not suited to use in the kitchen, are available which do cope with more humid summer climates). As lavenders originally come from limestone soil areas, it's advisable in acid soil areas to add lime or dolomite lime to the soils to increase soil alkalinity.

Growing in pots: lavenders are well suited to growing in pots, but do put the pots onto pot feet, to provide the good soil drainage they need. Slow-release fertiliser applied in spring is sufficient.

Best time to sow: plant seedlings in autumn or spring.

Picking tips: pick flowers in late spring or early summer; these can then be dried by hanging in a cool, airy place until dry, then used when needed. The leaves of English lavender, fresh or dried, are also useful in the kitchen. Dried lavenders will keep in air-tight containers for up to a year.

In the kitchen: lavender has a very strong flavour, so it is best when used sparingly. Create lavender sugars and lavender vinegars as a way of adding lavender flavours to sweet or savoury dishes.

Heaven with: a variety of sweet dishes, from biscuits to cakes, and also to flavour sugar used in making desserts. Lavender is also used in tandem with other Mediterreanean herbs (eg thyme, rosemary, sage) to flavour a variety of savoury foods.

Varieties: as well as growing *L. angustifolia* look for named hybrids such as 'Munstead', 'Hidcote Pink' and 'Hidcote'.

Lemon balm

Melissa officinalis

This spreading herb is highly valued for its lemony leaves, and it is so easy to grow that many gardeners consider it to be a weed. It comes from the same Lamiaceae family as mint, another wonderful tasting herb with a tendency to wander and take over garden beds. One lemon balm plant is all that's needed for starters, as it will multiply readily over time. Lemon balm (*Melissa officinalis*) is native to southern Europe and Western Asia, and now comes in many cultivars, some low-growing to just 30cm/1ft tall, more often they're taller, 60–100cm/2–3ft. Small yellow, white or pale purple flowers appear in summer. The leaves are heart-shaped, tooth-edged (like mint), crinkled and mid to dark green in colour, and strongly lemony in fragrance. Plants can die down in winter in cooler climate zones, reshooting in spring.

Growing tips: lemon balm grows readily from seeds or by divisions of existing plants. It prefers partial shade and isn't very fussy about soils, but can grow in full sun, too. As is the practice with its relative, mint, some gardeners seek to restrict its spread either by growing it in a pot, or planting into a pot that is then sunk into the ground (to control the spread of its roots).

Harvesting: young leaves are the ones to harvest, as they have a fresh, lemony flavour that the older leaves lose, and use them on the day you harvest them, too.

In the kitchen: think of all the dishes in which lemon flavours provide a boost and lemon balm can be used there: in salads and sauces, with chicken, fish and vegetables, in soups and desserts. Lemon balm's lemony flavour doesn't survive cooking very well, so use it at the last moment. Use it to make a herb butter, and to flavour vinegars. It goes very well with fruits such as apples, apricots, nectarines, peaches, melons and summer berries, and team it with vegetables such as carrots, mushrooms, tomatoes and zucchinis (courgettes). It also goes well with other herbs, such as chervil, chives, dill, fennel, ginger, mint and parsley.

Lemon balm tea: traditionally a 'calming' herb, lemon balm is used both as a tea on its own or as a flavouring for other teas. It aids sleep, and is often teamed with other calming herbs such as chamomile and valerian.

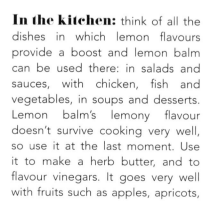

Lemon grass

Cymbopogon citratus

This tropical grass whose stalks possess a citrussy tang is a common ingredient in many South-East Asian cuisines, and it's also an attractive addition to the herb garden. With its long, green, grassy leaves, it grows to form a clump 1–1.2m/3–4ft high and 75cm/30in wide.

Growing basics: though it's native to tropical zones, lemon grass is capable of being grown in subtropical and temperate areas. In warmer areas it grows year-round, but frosty winters might kill plants, if frosts are severe. It needs well-drained soil and a sunny spot, plus regular watering and monthly liquid feeds to do well. Though it can be grown from seed, it is mostly grown from divisions of existing clumps, sold as seedlings. It can be planted at any time in tropical and subtropical zones, but in temperate areas plant it in spring.

Growing in pots: lemon grass grows well in pots, but it grows so well that it can fill a pot in one summer, after which it will need unpotting, dividing of the clump and repotting. In cooler zones, bringing potted lemon grass plants indoors for winter is a good option.

Picking tips: simply cut off stalks as needed at the base, with a sharp knife.

In the kitchen: lemon grass is used in many dishes, complementing chicken, fish, seafood, pork, vegetables and Asian herbs and spices very well. As lemon grass stalks are fairly tough, they are often very finely sliced crossways before being added to stir-fries, salad dressings and other dishes. Some cooks peel off the outer layers of the stalk to reveal the pink-tinged, more tender inner parts, then chop this finely. Alternatively, cooks will also leave the white lower part of the stalks whole then bruise it with a knife handle to release its lemony flavour, then add this to curries, soups and other dishes (it's then discarded before serving). Dried lemon grass has a poor flavour (use fresh lemon peel or leaves instead). Fresh lemon grass stalks will keep for two to three weeks in the refrigerator, and it also freezes well.

Lemon grass tea: this is a delightful plant to make tea from. Any part of the lemon grass stalk can be used to make tea, the leafy green tops or the white lower parts. You have the option of enjoying lemon grass as a light tea on its own, or as a flavouring for other teas, such as green teas.

Beef rendang

Serves 4

750g/24oz topside beef
4 tablespoons desiccated coconut
2 stalks lemon grass
2 onions, chopped
2 cloves garlic, chopped
5cm/2in piece ginger, chopped
2 red chillies, deseeded and sliced
2 tablespoons vegetable oil
1 teaspoon turmeric
400ml/14fl oz canned coconut milk
1 teaspoon sugar
salt

1 Trim any excess fat from the beef and cut into 2.5cm/1in cubes. Heat a large saucepan and dry-fry the coconut for 5 minutes or until golden, stirring frequently. Finely grind the coconut in a food processor.

2 Peel the outer layers from the lemon grass stalks, then finely chop the lower white bulbous parts, discarding the fibrous tops. Blend the lemon grass, onions, garlic, ginger and half the chilli to a paste. Heat the oil in the pan and fry the paste for 5 minutes to release the flavours, stirring often. Add the beef, stir to coat and fry for 3–4 minutes, until sealed.

3 Add the ground coconut, turmeric, coconut milk, sugar and salt, and mix well. Bring to the boil, stirring, then reduce the heat. Simmer, uncovered, for 3 hours, stirring from time to time, until the sauce reduces to a rich gravy. Garnish with the remaining chilli. Serve with rice.

Note This classic Indonesian dish can also be made with lamb or venison. Slow cooking in the rich coconut sauce results in meltingly tender meat.

Lemon myrtle

Backhousia citriodora

A great substitute for lemon grass or lemon rind, lemon myrtle leaves come from the Australian plant, *Backhousia citriodora*. Originally from the subtropical Queensland coastal regions, it's a dense, bushy shrub or small tree from 3–8m/10–26ft tall. It produces attractive sprays of white flowers in summer and autumn, but it's the evergreen foliage which is harvested for the kitchen. The tough leaves are edible but are usually not eaten whole.

Growing tips: this is a charming, fragrant garden plant, so it's well suited to growing near a pathway where you can brush past it and release its lemony scent. In temperate to tropical areas, lemon myrtle also is an excellent hedging plant. It's suited to tropical, subtropical and warm, frost-free temperate climates. Young plants are frost-tender. Once established it is a low-maintenance planting. The best way to grow it is from cuttings, rather than seed.

Growing in pots: lemon myrtle can be grown in pots, and it has even been grown successfully indoors. Like most Australian native plants, it is sensitive to both too much fertiliser and the wrong type of fertiliser, so use sparingly a slow-release food formulated for Australian native plants, one that is very low in phosphorus.

In the kitchen: the leaves, fresh or dried, have a strong lemon flavour and can be used with seafood or chicken dishes, and to flavour cakes and desserts. However, as the flavour is strong, don't add too much. Dried lemon myrtle leaves are now sold as a flavouring for fish, seafood and other meats. The classic 'lemon pepper' dry seasoning used to flavour Mediterranean meat and seafood barbecues now has its Australian bushfood equivalent, it being a blend of lemon myrtle and native pepperberry (*Tasmannia lanceolata*). The general rule with using lemon myrtle is that it can be used wherever a recipe requires lemon flavouring, but as it suits shorter cooking rather than long cooking, try it first in stir-fries, in marinades or rubs for barbecued meats, chicken, seafood or vegetables, in dipping sauces and salad dressings.

Dried lemon myrtle: drying intensifies the flavour of lemon myrtle, so use this sparingly if the recipe specifies fresh leaves. To dry fresh leaves, harvest the darker, more mature leaves, tie in a bunch then hang in a dry, airy place for several days.

Lemon myrtle tea: either fresh or dried lemon myrtle leaves can be added to tea, but as its flavour is relatively strong it's best to be sparing at first when experimenting with it. Use just a little to flavour green tea.

Lemon verbena

Aloysia citriodora

Native to Chile and Argentina in South America, lemon verbena is a 1–3m/3–10ft tall perennial shrub with superbly fragrant, lemon-scented foliage. For that reason alone it's worth growing in any garden, but its lemon-flavoured foliage also has many uses in the kitchen.

Growing basics: lemon verbena prefers warm climates and doesn't like frosts, so it's grown outdoors only in warm, temperate zones and the subtropics and tropics. A position in full sun with well-drained soil is essential, and summer humidity is not a problem. Plants can be started from seed sown in spring, or propagated from soft-tip cuttings taken in spring from the new growth on established plants. Alternatively, semi-hardwood cuttings can be taken in late summer or early autumn. Plants grown from cuttings may be slow to get started, so don't rush planting them out into the garden. Established plants will benefit from an all-over trim in autumn (but not hard cutting back).

Growing in pots: you can grow lemon verbena in a large pot, and in cooler climates some gardeners bring their potted lemon verbenas in under shelter during the cooler months.

Picking tips: just take fresh leaves as needed. Leaves can also be frozen in ice cubes for use later on in drinks or cooking.

In the kitchen: wherever you need a lemon flavour in cooking, lemon verbena can supply it, and the lemon flavour of the leaves survives cooking well. It goes very well with fish and poultry, pork and duck. It complements vegetables such as carrots and zucchini (courgettes), and teams well with rice in pilaffs. It also has many uses in sweet desserts, especially those based on fruit, and a small scattering of a finely chopped leaf can transform a garden salad. It also teams well with other herbs, such as basil, chives, chilli, coriander and mint.

Lemon verbena tea: both fresh lemon verbena leaves and dried leaves, which retain much of the original flavour, can be used in making tea. To make tea, pour one cup of water over ¼ cup fresh leaves, or half that amount of dried leaves. Strain and pour after five minutes.

Licorice

Glycyrrhiza glabra

Originally from the Mediterranean region, the Middle-East and western Asia, licorice (*Glycyrrhiza glabra*) is a 1m/3ft tall perennial legume which has been valued as a breath freshener and sweet cooking ingredient since ancient times (licorice roots were found in the tomb of the Egyptian Pharaoh, Tutankhamen). It's the peeled, dried roots of the plant, harvested after three to five years' growth, which are the valuable crop. The main chemical in the roots is the intensely sweet glycyrrhizin, which is 30 to 50 times sweeter than regular sugar. Its main commercial growing areas are Russia, Iran, Spain and India.

Growing tips: licorice is a herbaceous perennial about 1m/3ft tall in the garden. Its pale blue to violet flowers in spring are followed by seedpods. While licorice can be grown in many climate zones, it does best in a climate with lots of winter rain and summer dryness and sunshine, and it can handle severe winter frosts down to -12°C/10°F. It does best in good quality, well-drained, alkaline soil. Plants can be started from either seed or a piece of root.

Harvesting: autumn is harvest time, when these deciduous plants start to die down for winter. Plants are dug up entirely (though growers save some of the crown and suckers to replant in the following spring). Though the very sweet root, which is bright yellow when cut, can be chewed fresh, eating too much is not advisable, as it can make you very ill (with side-effects such as headaches and high blood pressure). Most licorice is turned into an extract, by crushing the roots to a pulp, which is then boiled, then the extract is produced via evaporation.

In the kitchen: with its very sweet taste licorice has many uses in the manufacturing of more than just foods, flavouring everything from cough syrups and toothpaste through to beers and cigarettes. Of course it is well loved for its uses in make confectionery, ranging from the licorice allsorts popular in Europe through to licorice sticks which people in many Asian countries like to chew on. In the kitchen, it is often used as a powder, and its slightly aniseedy sweetness combines well with other spices such as cassia, cloves, coriander, fennel, ginger and star anise. Too much licorice will give a bitter aftertaste, so use it sparingly.

Lovage

Levisticum officinale

This tall-growing (2m/6ft) perennial herb is well worth growing in your herb garden but put it towards the back of the bed where it won't overshadow the smaller plants. Native to Western Asia and Southern Europe, lovage is related to parsley and sometimes it is called love parsley or sea parsley. That's because its leaves look like flat-leaf continental parsley, but its flavour is closer to that of celery. This is a perennial plant which will last for many years in the garden, growing 2m/6ft tall and spreading 1m/3ft wide. Its flowers are tiny and greenish yellow, and these are followed by large seed heads bearing many seeds.

Growing basics: lovage has naturalised in many temperate climate zones around the world, and that's the climate to which it is best suited. Seeds can be sown in autumn or spring, but you can also divide an established plant in spring and plant that, for a faster start. Lovage likes rich, moist, well-drained soil in a spot that's either sunny or at least has partial sun during the day. It dies down in winter, so in late autumn plants can be cut back hard, and they will reshoot in the following spring.

Growing in pots: lovage can be grown successfully in a large, deep pot, but in a pot it will look much better if clipped back regularly to maintain a denser, smaller size.

Picking tips: the new growth in spring and early summer has the best flavour. The seeds can be harvested and dried in autumn, for use in the kitchen. To dry seeds, cut off the seed heads, place in a paper bag and hang it up in a dry spot until the seeds fall out into the bag.

In the kitchen: the primary flavour of lovage is that of celery, so it can be used as a celery substitute, which gives it many uses in soups, sauces, stews and stocks. Lovage has a much stronger flavour than celery, so use it in moderation. It is sometimes also used as a parsley substitute, and again moderation is advisable. It goes well with vegetables such as potatoes, carrots, corn and root vegetables, and it combines well with other herbs and spices, including bay, caraway, chilli, chives, dill, oregano, parsley and thyme.

Medicinal benefits: though not used to make tea, research shows that lovage is a diuretic, and it can also help to ease digestive tract problems.

Marigolds

Calendula and *Tagetes*

Several popular garden flowers are known as 'marigolds' but only a few have uses in the kitchen. The pretty orange-coloured petals of the pot marigold, *Calendula officinalis*, are tossed into summer salads as a colourful edible garnish. The other marigolds with some uses in the kitchen belong to the genus *Tagetes*. The Mexican marigold, *T. lucida*, is a perennial which is sometimes called Mexican tarragon. The French marigold, *T. patula*, is an annual whose flower petals are also edible. Another plant, *T. minuta*, is a taller-growing (1–2m/3–6ft) annual which plays an important role in Peruvian cuisine, where it is known as huacatay or black mint.

Growing basics: all these marigolds do best in well-drained soil in a sunny spot. For winter and spring flowers in temperate zones, pot marigold (*Calendula*) can be grown from seed sown in autumn (seedlings are also available). For summer flowers, seeds or seedlings of French marigolds can be sown in spring. Mexican marigolds are grown for their leaves, and are planted as seedlings, in spring.

Growing in pots: both pot marigolds and French marigolds are very suitable choices for pots, either on their own or to bring some flower colour to a mixed planting of herbs.

In the kitchen: as well as using the fresh flower petals of pot and French marigolds as a garnish for garden salads, the dried, ground petals of French marigolds are used as a flavouring and colouring in various Eastern European cuisines and those of the Caucasus (where it is referred to as Imeretian saffron). Mexican marigold petals are used in Central American and Indigenous American cuisines, where its tarragon-like aniseed flavour goes well with vegetables, fish and chicken. The South American marigold called Huacatay has a strongly aromatic flavour that is used in potato dishes, in soups, stews and on grilled meats.

Medicinal benefits: *Tyler's Honest Herbal* says that most of the health benefit claims for pot marigolds are unproven, but there is good evidence it does help in the healing of wounds, one of the traditional benefits claimed for it. Marigold tea is popular both to drink and, when cool, to apply topically to wounds.

Mint

Mentha spicata

Most mints belong to the genus *Mentha*. Plant sizes vary, but many grow 20–40cm/8–18in high and spread vigorously. There are many different mints. All are perennial which can live in the garden for many years. Plants can have white, pink or mauve flowers, in late summer or autumn.

Growing basics: mint thrives in damp soil and partial shade. This herb should be grown in a pot, not in the ground as it sprawls and can take over a garden bed quickly. Plants can become sparse and 'leggy' in shade, so cut back regularly to maintain bushiness.

Growing in pots: a wide, shallow pot is a better choice for mint. Water pots very regularly, especially in hot weather.

Best time to sow: mint is not usually grown from seed. Seedlings or cuttings are the best way to get started. Cuttings will form roots rapidly in a glass of water and can be planted out then.

Picking tips: just pick as required, either harvesting leaves with fingers or whole stems with scissors.

In the kitchen: mint is best used fresh. In stir-fries it can be a substitute for coriander. Dried mint is not a good substitute for fresh mint, however. Fresh mint can be kept in good condition for a few days by placing it in a glass of water, and keeping this in the refrigerator.

Success secrets: plenty of water is essential, so too monthly liquid feeds. Regular harvesting will keep plants compact and bushy.

Heaven with: lamb, chicken, pork and veal. It is used to flavour teas, and complements many vegetables and salads. Add finely chopped mint to yoghurt for a simple, tangy sauce. Mint goes very well with many fruits, including mangoes and strawberries. Its cooling qualities make it popular in sambals, chutneys and sauces in spicy Thai and Indian cuisines.

Varieties: common mint, peppermint, spearmint, apple mint, eau de cologne mint, chocolate mint and many others. Each variety's flavour varies, but common mint and spearmint are good choices if you're starting out. Spearmint has a refreshing toothpaste-style flavour, while peppermint is spicy, and chocolate mint tastes like after dinner mints. 'Taste test' before buying any mint, as their flavours vary markedly.

Not mints: Vietnamese mint isn't a mint (it's *Periscaria odorata*) nor is Korean mint (*Agastache rugosa*).

Pictured left: spearmint

Crab rice paper rolls

Makes about 22

60g/2oz vermicelli noodles
1 Lebanese cucumber, halved lengthwise
    and seeds removed
4 scallions/spring onions, thinly sliced
½ bunch cilantro/coriander, leaves picked
½ bunch fresh mint, leaves picked
300g/10½oz fresh cooked crab meat (or 2 cups
    shredded cooked chicken)
¼ cup lemon juice
2 tablespoons sweet chilli sauce
22 small rice paper sheets (about 16cm/6in round)

Dipping Sauce
¼ cup sweet chilli sauce
2 tablespoons rice vinegar
2 teaspoons fish sauce

1 Cook noodles in a saucepan of boiling water for 3–4 minutes or until tender. Drain and set aside. Cut cucumber in half again lengthwise and thinly slice.

2 Combine noodles, spring onions, cucumber, coriander, mint, crab meat, lemon juice and sweet chilli sauce in a bowl. Dip each rice paper sheet in a bowl of very hot water (nearly boiling) until soft. Place four at a time on a clean surface. Place spoonfuls of the crab mixture on the sheets, fold in the edges and roll up. Repeat with remaining mixture and sheets.

3 To make the dipping sauce, combine sweet chilli sauce, rice vinegar and fish sauce in a small bowl.

Mountain pepper

Tasmannia lanceolata

This Australian native pepper is also known as bush pepper or pepperberry. Both the leaves and dried berries of the small evergreen tree or shrub, *Tasmannia lanceolata*, have an aromatic, peppery flavour. The mountain pepper plant is native to damp, higher-elevation areas and rainforest gullies of Tasmania and up along Australia's East Coast. It forms a shrub or small tree 2–4m/6–13ft tall (in gardens, but up to 10m/33ft in the wild) with smooth, green, lance-shaped leaves (which look like bay leaves) and distinctive red stems. White, pale yellow or cream flowers in summer are followed by pea-sized red berries which fully ripen to black in autumn. There are separate male and female plants, so you'll need both to produce a good crop of berries.

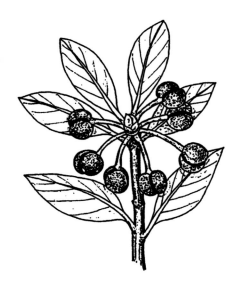

Growing basics: this is grown as a garden plant in Australia, as its red leaf stalks and stems look good, and the autumn berries attract native birds. It can be grown from seeds or cuttings, but cuttings are the most common method, and it needs a moist, well-drained acid soil in a sheltered position in full sun to part shade. The ideal climate is cool to cold temperate.

Growing in pots: this can be grown in a pot, but as it needs constantly moist soil, good watering during hot, dry summer weather is essential.

In the kitchen: crushed mountain pepper berries have a stronger pepper flavour than black pepper, so use less of it when using it as a substitute. The fresh leaves of this plant can be used in cooking to impart a peppery flavour, and the dried leaves have an even stronger flavour. Most cooks use the berries, whole or crushed, and these can be used in all the ways pepper is used, in soups, stocks, casseroles, stews and other slow-cooked dishes. This pungent pepper suits robust flavoured meats such as game, beef and lamb, and strongly flavoured vegetables including legumes, root vegetables and pumpkin. Mountain pepper is often blended in with other spices and herbs, including lemon myrtle, lemon thyme, thyme, marjoram, oregano, rosemary and wattleseed.

Heaven with: dried, crushed lemon myrtle leaves combined with crushed mountain pepper makes a superb spice rub for grilled chicken or fish.

Mustard

Brassica spp.

Valued mostly as a spicy condiment but also as a peppery salad herb, mustard comes from plants which are fast-growing annuals, originally from Europe and Asia Minor, all members of the genus *Brassica*. Mustard, the popular spicy condiment, is based on mustard seeds, of which there are three main types. Black mustard seed comes from *B. nigra*; white or yellow mustard seed from *B. alba*; and brown mustard seed from *B. juncea*. Black and brown mustard seeds have a stronger, more pungent flavour than white seeds. Mustard seed oil is also widely used in Indian cookery.

Growing tips: mustard plants grow best in temperate climates in summer, but can also be grown in subtropical zones. They need full sun and well-drained soil and grow best from seed, which germinates quickly when sown in spring.

Harvesting tips: though some plants will grow 75cm/30in tall when mature (at which point they flower in summer and set seed), mustard plants grown as a salad herb are harvested when much smaller, 15–20cm/6–8in tall. To harvest seeds, let plants grow to their full size, then flower and set seed. Cut off seed pods when fully developed but before they split open. To collect the seeds, put pods in paper bags, hang these up until the pods are dry.

Growing in pots: mustard plants can be grown successfully in pots, and some varieties with coloured leaves are very decorative.

In the kitchen: fresh mustard leaves for a salad of mixed greens should be small, and as they are peppery in flavour only a few are needed each time. Mustard leaves lose their bite when cooked and are often included in South-East Asian stir-fries. Mustard seeds have many uses in cookery. In Indian cuisines they are part of the widely used seed mix, panch phoron (brown or black mustard, fennel, nigella, fenugreek and cumin) which is fried in oil at the start of cooking. Mustard seeds on their own are also often fried in oil to flavour the oil. Seeds are also ground to make curry pastes, and in many cuisines they are an important pickling spice. Mustard oil is also a key flavour in Indian cookery, bringing a piquant flavour and aroma to dishes. Prepared mustards are usually manufactured, and each reflects either its region or country of origin, so there are French, English, German and US mustards, along with regional types such as Dijon, Bordeaux and many others.

Heaven with: steak and prawns; sausages and hot dogs wouldn't be the same without your favourite mustard; also try French mustard and tarragon next time you're cooking chicken.

Nasturtium

Tropaeolum majus

This easy-care, pretty little flowering plant is edible and both the leaves and flowers can be added to salads. Its names are a source of confusion, as it is sometimes called Indian cress but is not related to watercress. And though it's called nasturtium it doesn't belong to the genus *Nasturtium*, to which watercress belongs. What it does have in common with other cresses is that it's peppery in flavour and that it's so easy to grow it's a weed in many areas. Flowers, produced in summer and autumn, are often orange and leaves mid-green, but red and yellow blooms are common, as are forms with variegated leaves. Varieties with semi-double and double flowers are also available, and forms vary from low-spreading trailers through to compact dwarfs and small climbers. It's originally from the Andes Mountains of South America.

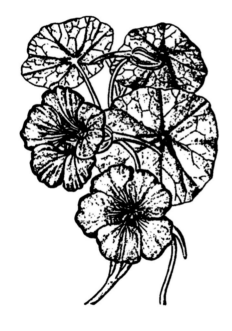

Growing basics: nasturtiums are annuals which grow very easily from seed in spots ranging from sunny to semi-shaded, but it will flower best in full sun. It prefers moist, fertile soil, but doesn't like frosty conditions, growing best during spring, summer and autumn in temperate zones. Plants can be started from seed or seedlings, and as the seeds are large and easy to handle, they are a good plant for children to grow. In warm, frost-free areas seeds can be sown in spring and autumn, but in frost-prone areas sow seeds in spring only. No fertiliser is needed, and in fact fertilising can result in more foliage and fewer flowers. Pick flowers regularly to prolong flowering.

Growing in pots: nasturtiums can grow in pots, but with their spreading habit they suit a wide, shallow pot best.

Picking tips: just pick leaves and flowers as needed, but the more you pick the flowers the more flowers plants will produce.

In the kitchen: nasturtiums have fairly limited uses in the kitchen, most appearing in mixed green salads. The leaves have a peppery flavour rather like watercress, so should be used sparingly, while the flowers have a milder flavour and make a very pretty garnish for a salad. The immature, small round seeds and unopened flower buds can be pickled then used as a substitute for capers.

Smoked chicken pappardelle with nasturtium butter

Serves 4

500g/1lb pappardelle
300g/10oz smoked chicken breast, sliced
½ cup white wine
1 cup thickened cream
½ bunch fresh chives, chopped
freshly ground black pepper

Nasturtium Butter
10 nasturtium flowers
125g/4oz butter, softened
1 clove garlic, crushed
1 tablespoon lime juice

1 To make nasturtium butter, finely chop half the flowers and place in a bowl with the butter, garlic and lime juice, mix well to combine and set aside.

2 Bring a large saucepan of salted water to the boil, add the pasta and cook for 8 minutes or until just firm in the centre (al dente). Drain, set aside and keep warm.

3 Heat a non-stick frying pan over a medium heat, add chicken and cook, stirring, for 1 minute. Add wine, cream, chives and black pepper and simmer for 4 minutes to reduce. To serve, top pasta with chicken mixture and nasturtium butter and garnish with remaining whole flowers.

Nettle

Urtica spp.

Famous for their leaves, which can deliver a sharp sting when handled, nettles are, oddly enough, both edible and healthy, and useful in herbal medicine. There are several different nettles, the most common of which is the stinging nettle, *Urtica dioica*, a hardy perennial weed found in many countries which spreads readily via its creeping roots. In some species of stinging nettles there are distinct male and female plants: the flowers of the female plants are tiny and hang down in clusters while the (also tiny) male flowers poke out from the plant. Its tooth-edged green leaves are covered in stinging bristles, even when young.

Growing basics: position plants in their own corner where people can't come in contact with them. The plants themselves aren't fussy about soils. They can be grown from either seed or a piece of root, planted in spring, which will spread rapidly without encouragement.

Growing in pots: nettles aren't suited to pots.

Picking tips: it's only the fresh, small top leaves of new nettle shoots which are harvested in spring for the kitchen. You must wear gloves and a long-sleeve shirt when working about nettle plants. In herbal medicine, the entire plants are harvested just before flowering commences. *Warning*: don't harvest leaves from public areas likely to have been sprayed with weedkillers.

In the kitchen: before handling nettle leaves, the 'sting' in them must first be neutralised by blanching them (minus stalks) in boiling water for 10 minutes, then plunging the blanched leaves into iced water. They are then safe to handle. A traditional favourite recipe is to make a nettle soup, combining blanched nettles with vegetables, fresh herbs, stock and milk. Nettle leaves are also cooked and eaten in much the same way as spinach, as they are high in Vitamin C and carotene. No part of a nettle plant should be eaten raw, as there is a serious risk of poisoning, and kidney damage, if older plants are eaten uncooked.

Medicinal benefits: Dr Varro Tyler, in his book, *Tyler's Honest Herbal* says generations of bald men have applied stinging nettle juice to their heads in the hope of stimulating some hair growth. Alas, it doesn't work, nor is there much evidence to back up its uses in treating asthma and rheumatism. However, there is plenty of evidence to back nettle's usefulness as a diuretic and in helping to treat urinary problems with male prostate disease.

Nigella

Nigella sativa

The pretty blue or white garden flower with the fine, feathery leaves called 'love in a mist' is a form of Nigella (*N. damascena*). However, the plant grown for its spicy black seeds, *N. sativa*, is not quite as glamorous, although it does produce smallish white or blue flowers which are followed by the large seed pods. It's the small, angular black seeds that provide an earthy, peppery, bitter flavour much used in the cooking of the Indian subcontinent and elsewhere.

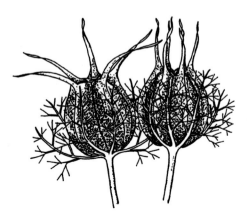

Growing basics: nigella is a flowering annual plant native to southern and south-western Asia. It grows to 30cm/1ft tall in a position in full sun and well-drained soil. Sow seed in spring in temperate and subtropical climates (where some protection via afternoon shade will help). Make sure to water plants regularly, and especially during any dry periods. Nigella produces a lot of seed and grows a bit too readily in fact, often self-seeding readily in subsequent years after the first crop is planted. So it is a potential weed.

Growing in pots: nigella grows easily in pots.

Picking tips: as plants are grown for seed collection, wait until after flowering finishes and seed pods have developed. Aim to harvest the pods before they start to split; pull out the whole plant, cover the seed pods in brown paper bags, and let them dry until they split and seeds fall out.

In the kitchen: nigella is a key component of the widely used Indian seed mix called panch phoron (meaning 'five seeds')

comprising in equal quantities of nigella, black or brown mustard, fenugreek, fennel and cumin. This seed mix is fried in hot oil at the start of cooking, to flavour the oil. Nigella seeds are often sprinkled on top of breads and savoury pastries prior to baking, often in tandem with sesame and/or cumin seed. In Indian cuisine, nigella is part of many spice mixes, teaming well with allspice, cardamom, cinnamon, coriander, cumin, fennel, pepper and turmeric. In Middle-Eastern cuisines it's often ground up with cumin and coriander to flavour everything from vegetable dishes to potatoes and omelettes.

Confusing names: nigella is often mis-named even on some spice packet labels. You'll often found it sold as 'black onion seed' (which it resembles) and also as 'black cumin seed' (which it doesn't particularly resemble). In Indian spice shops you'll often see it labelled as 'kalonji'.

Seared tuna salad with crisp wontons

Serves 4–6

Dressing

120ml/4fl oz olive oil

60ml/2fl oz lime juice

60ml/2fl oz orange juice

75ml/2½fl oz soy sauce

75ml/2½fl oz rice vinegar

1 tablespoon toasted sesame oil

½ bunch fresh chives, minced

1 tablespoon fresh ginger, minced

salt and pepper, to taste

Salad

1–2 tablespoons peanut oil

1 small red chilli, minced

8 spring onions, finely sliced on the diagonal

100g/3½oz baby corn

145g/5oz snow peas, trimmed

4 tablespoons sesame seeds

4 tablespoons nigella seeds

4 x 145g/5oz tuna steaks

salt and pepper, to taste

vegetable oil for deep-frying

8 wonton wrappers, cut into thin strips

1 To make the dressing, whisk the olive oil, lime juice, orange juice, soy sauce, rice vinegar, sesame oil, chives and ginger in small bowl to blend. Season with salt and pepper, to taste.

2 Heat the peanut oil in a wok and add the chilli, scallions, baby corn and snow peas, tossing over a high heat until the vegetables are crisp tender (about 3 minutes). Transfer the hot vegetables to a bowl and drizzle over a little of the dressing. Set aside.

3 Mix the sesame seeds and nigella seeds on a flat plate and season the tuna with salt and pepper. Press the tuna into the seed mixture, coating both sides evenly. Heat a little more oil in the same wok used for the vegetables. Add the tuna and sear over a high heat until just cooked through. Transfer to a platter and, when cool, use a sharp knife to slice each fillet thinly.

4 Heat some vegetable oil in a wok and, when smoking, add the strips of wonton and cook until golden brown. Remove from the wok and drain on absorbent paper. Add salt to taste.

5 Toss the lettuce leaves with the cooked vegetable mixture and a little more dressing, tossing thoroughly so the leaves are well coated. Add salt and pepper to taste. Divide the lettuce mixture among 4 plates and top with the tuna slices. Arrange a bundle of fried wonton strips on top.

Nutmeg & mace

Myristica fragrans

These two spices not only come from the same tropical plant (*Myristica fragrans*), they both come from the fruit of the plant. Cut through the fleshy outer part of the plant's apricot-sized fruit and you encounter the core, which contains the brown nutmeg seed, surrounded by a brilliant red, lacy covering, which is the mace. Both spices have similar but subtly different flavours. The original home to these trees was the Molucca Islands (in Indonesia) but now trees are grown in other tropical countries, including Grenada in the Caribbean, a major producer of these spices.

Growing tips: *M. fragrans* is an evergreen, equatorial tree which can only be grown successfully in humid equatorial regions. Needing a rich, moist, volcanic soil, these trees grow to 12–20m/38–66ft and both male and female trees are needed to produce fruit. In plantations, each tree takes about seven years to produce its first, small crop. So, they aren't suited to home cultivation in most areas.

Harvesting: when the fruits start to split they are ripe, then harvested and split open fully. The lacy red mace is removed and dried. The kernel itself is also dried until the seed (the nutmeg) starts to rattle loosely around inside it, at which stage the seed is opened and the nutmeg removed.

In the kitchen: freshly grated nutmeg is far superior in flavour to the powdered form, and nutmeg graters are available in good kitchenware stores; some graters are designed to be used at the dining table. So, nutmeg is best bought whole and grated fresh, although powdered nutmeg is readily available and commonly used. With its warm aroma it has many uses in spice mixes in cuisines ranging from North Africa and the Mediterranean all the way across to India. In European cookery nutmeg often teams with honey in sweet dishes, fruit cakes and fruit desserts. In savoury cooking the Italians add nutmeg to vegetable dishes and pasta sauces, and it teams with many vegetables very well, notably cabbage, potato, pumpkin and sweet potato, and it complements chicken, lamb, veal and fish. Nutmeg is cheaper and more plentiful and is the more widely used of the two spices.

Whole, dried, uncrushed strips of mace are referred to as 'blades' but you are most likely to come across this spice in powdered form. Mace costs more than nutmeg, so it's not as commonly used as its sister spice.

Baby spinach tarts

Makes 20

Pastry
1½ cups plain flour
4 tablespoons grated parmesan cheese
125g/4oz butter, chopped

Spinach Filling
2 teaspoons olive oil
2 spring onions, chopped
1 clove garlic, crushed
8 spinach leaves, shredded
125g/4oz ricotta cheese, drained
2 eggs, lightly beaten
⅓ cup milk
½ teaspoon grated nutmeg
4 tablespoons pine nuts

1 Preheat oven to 200°C/400°F. To make pastry, place flour, parmesan cheese and butter in a food processor and process until mixture resembles fine breadcrumbs.

2 With machine running, slowly add 2–3 tablespoons of iced water to form a soft dough. Turn dough onto a lightly floured surface and knead briefly. Wrap dough in cling wrap and refrigerate for 30 minutes.

3 Roll out pastry to 3mm/0.1in thick. Using an 8cm/3in fluted pastry cutter, cut out 20 pastry rounds. Place pastry rounds in lightly greased patty tins. Pierce base and sides of pastry with a fork and bake for 5–10 minutes or until lightly golden. Reduce oven temperature to 180°C/350°F.

4 To make filling, heat oil in a frying pan over a medium heat. Add spring onions, garlic and spinach and cook, stirring, until spinach is wilted. Remove pan from heat and set aside to cool.

5 Place spinach mixture, ricotta cheese, eggs, milk and nutmeg in a bowl and mix to combine. Spoon filling into pastry cases, sprinkle with pine nuts and bake for 15–20 minutes or until tarts are golden and filling is set.

Oregano & marjoram

Origanum vulgare, O. majorana

These two herbs are grouped together not only because both are species of *Origanum* but they also have the same growing needs. Both are worth adding to your herb garden, as oregano has a stronger flavour which is useful in certain dishes, and the milder flavour of marjoram makes it its own distinct cooking ingredient. These herbs are low, bushy perennials with a spreading habit, growing 45cm/18in high and spreading 90cm/3ft. Common oregano (*Origanum vulgare*) leaves are oval, mid-green and hairy underneath, the stems are red-tinged, and the flowers can be purplish-pink or white. Sweet marjoram (*O. majorana*) leaves are grey-green, its stems are light coloured and the flowers are white.

Growing basics: both plants like full sun and well-drained soil; apply a liquid food monthly during the main growing period in late spring and summer. Oregano is generally longer-lived than marjoram; in fact marjoram is often grown as an annual plant.

Growing in pots: low, wide shallow pots, one plant per pot, are best suited to their spreading growth habit. Let the potting mix dry out between waterings, although increase watering during hot summers.

Best time to sow: sow seed in spring or autumn; established clumps of oregano can be dug up, divided and replanted in early spring. Marjoram is often grown as an annual, from seed or seedlings (which are readily available for many months).

Picking tips: harvest leaves as needed; the leaves of both plants dry and retain their flavour well, so if you have an excess or need to cut plants back, dry the leaves and store them in a sealed jar for use in the kitchen.

In the kitchen: either fresh or dried oregano and marjoram are useful kitchen herbs; it depends on what the recipe requires. Oregano is a basic ingredient in many Greek marinades and sauces, in Italian pasta sauces, and in countless herb and spice blends. Marjoram, with its milder flavour, is best added towards the end of cooking, while oregano's stronger flavour can cope with the long, slow cooking needed in soups and casseroles.

Heaven with: oregano goes very well with potatoes and many other vegetables, chicken, lamb and veal. It's superb with tomatoes and tomato sauces. Marjoram goes well in salads, fish and poultry but try it also with milder flavoured cheeses and cheese sauces.

Varieties: as well as common oregano and marjoram, there is a golden variety of oregano which looks very pretty in the garden, and is good in the kitchen.

Pictured left: marjoram
Pictured right: oregano

Baby octopus marinated in olive oil and oregano

Serves 4

¹/₃ cup olive oil
zest of 1 lemon, grated
2 tablespoons lemon juice
¹/₃ cup spring onions, finely sliced
2 teaspoons oregano, chopped
salt and freshly ground black pepper
750g/24oz baby octopus, cleaned
salad leaves, for serving

1 In a bowl, mix together the olive oil, lemon zest, lemon juice, spring onions, oregano, and pepper and salt. Add the octopus, and leave to marinate for 1 hour.

2 Heat a chargrill pan, lightly brush with oil, add octopus, and cook, basting with marinade for 2–3 minutes, or until tender. Serve on a bed of salad leaves.

Pandan

Pandanus amaryllifolius, P. tectorius

The leaves of this tropical tree are used in many ways in the crafts, clothing and housing of Pacific island cultures, and they are also used to flavour and wrap foods throughout the tropics and subtropics. There are more than 600 species of *Pandanus*, but *P. tectorius* and *P. amaryllifolius* are grown most commonly. *P. tectorius* is also called the screwpine and coastal breadfruit, due to the pineapple-like fruit the female plants produce.

Growing basics: pandanus grows best in full sun and thrives in seaside areas in the tropics and subtropics. Once established, it needs no extra watering and is easy-care. Tree sizes vary from 2–20m/6–66ft tall, depending on the variety. *P. tectorius* is 4–14m/13–45ft tall, and its base spreads as it sends down 'stilt roots' which help to stabilise the tree. A 6m/20ft wide canopy of long (90–150cm/3–5ft) strap-like leaves also forms.

Growing in pots: small pandanus species can be grown in large pots.

Planting: you can germinate fresh seeds sown in pots of moist, sandy potting mix (germination can be slow). Large branches can also be used as cuttings in spring if allowed to dry at the base then planted into a sandy mix.

In the kitchen: pandan leaves need to be scraped to release their delicate flavour, and one way to use them is to tear one into strips, tie a strip into a knot and toss it into a rice pot. The flavour released is fresh and floral. Leaves are used to flavour sweet sticky rice desserts, plus spicy soups and curries in South-East Asian cuisines. Leaves are also used to wrap foods to be cooked, such as rice or chicken parcels, and skilful hands can weave pandan strips into little serving baskets. Use pandan leaves to flavour chicken, rice or coconut dishes and curries, and combine it with chilli, coriander leaves, galangal, ginger, lemon grass and Thai lime. An essence made from pandanus flowers, called kewra essence, gives a mild pandan flavour, and powdered pandan and dried and frozen leaves are also available, none of which match the fresh product for fragrance or flavour. Pandan fruits are a traditional food throughout the Pacific Islands, either eaten fresh as a fruit, or cooked and mixed to a paste with coconut milk, then baked as little cakes.

Names: in Sri Lanka pandan is rampe; in Indonesia and Malaysia it is daun pandan; In Thailand it is bai toey; in Vietnam, la dua.

Paprika

Capsicum annuum

Elsewhere in this book you will find chillies also listed as being derived from *Capsicum annuum*, and it's a testament to this plant's versatility that it also needs an entry for the powdered product make from its fruit, paprika, as this is a very different ingredient in the kitchen. Several countries have their own versions of paprika, and each is unique to its country of origin. Notable paprika-makers are Hungary, Spain, Portugal, and Balkan states such as Bosnia and Serbia.

Growing basics: see our entry on chillies on page 70 for our growing tips, if you want to grow chillies, but to grow plants for your own paprika the problem is not the growing, it's the processing of the fruits which makes this a difficult exercise at home.

Making paprika: chilli fruits are harvested and dried, then the internal parts of the fruit (seeds and veins) are separated and ground separately, then re-blended in different amounts to make paprika. Each type of paprika may also come from one or more varieties of chillies. Many Spanish paprikas are notable for their smoky flavour, some Hungarian paprikas have a distinctly higher level of heat, and the 'sweet' paprika used commonly in English-speaking kitchens is mild in flavour and has no heat.

In the kitchen: using the correct paprika from the country of origin is essential if an authentic flavour is desired, and often these can only be found by visiting a specialist delicatessen for that cuisine, or by shopping online from a specialist supplier. That said, you'll need paprika to make Hungarian goulash (or a Balkan goulash). In Spanish cuisine paprika is a key ingredient in making sofrito, an essential flavour base made at the start of many dishes, and it's a key flavouring in chorizo and other sausages. Paprika forms part of many North African spice blends. It goes very well with most meats and vegetables and combines with an equally wide range of spices. Mild sweet paprika is also an important component of barbecue rubs for meat, teaming with brown sugar, garlic powder, onion powder, salt and pepper. Instead of making their own paprika, good cooks concentrate on getting the 'right' paprika for the recipe at hand.

What is pimiento? It's another capsicum product, much used in Spanish cuisine, made from round, red capsicums, which can be hot or mild. Sometimes used fresh, they are often pickled and sold in jars or cans. They are the red peppers used to stuff green olives.

Hungarian goulash soup

Serves 4

3 tablespoons olive oil

2 medium white onions, sliced

2 tablespoons Hungarian (mild) paprika

2 cloves garlic, minced

2 teaspoons caraway seeds

8 sprigs fresh marjoram, leaves removed and stalks
    discarded

500g/1lb diced beef

400g/14oz canned diced tomatoes

2 tablespoons tomato paste

6 cups beef stock

2 teaspoons brown sugar

1 teaspoon salt

1 teaspoon pepper

400g/14oz potatoes, diced

200g/7oz carrots, diced

1 tablespoon cornflour, mixed with 2 tablespoons
    cold water

¼ cup sour cream

2 pickled cucumbers, finely diced

3 cooked Frankfurters, finely sliced (optional)

1 Heat the olive oil in a saucepan and sauté the onion until golden brown, about 5 minutes. Add the paprika, garlic, caraway seeds and marjoram and cook for 1–2 minutes until the mixture is fragrant.

2 Add the beef, diced tomatoes and tomato paste, and cook until the meat is well coated and is a rich brown colour, about 5 minutes. Add the stock, sugar, salt and pepper and bring to the boil. Simmer for 1 hour. Add the potatoes and carrots and continue cooking for a further 30 minutes.

3 Check seasonings and adjust if necessary. Stir the cornflour mixture into the soup, mixing well. Allow the soup to thicken for a couple of minutes, then serve in individual bowls.

4 Garnish with sour cream, cucumbers and Frankfurters, if using.

Parsley

Petroselinum crispum

This popular biannual herb is *Petroselinum crispum*. 'Biannual' means that it can live through two growing seasons, but in many gardens it is still grown and treated as a longer-lived annual. Two main types are grown: the flat-leafed form known variously as Italian or Continental parsley, and the crinkle-leafed form commonly called curly parsley. The flat-leafed form has gained favour with cooks, while the milder-flavoured curly-leafed form is preferred as a decorative garnish, although it is still a useful kitchen herb. Flat-leaf parsley is a slightly bigger plant (around 30cm/1ft tall) than more compact curly parsley.

Growing basics: parsley grows well in semi-shade to full sun in fertile, well-drained soil. Sowing parsley seed is a more reliable way to get started, but seeds can take three to four weeks to germinate (soaking seed in hot water prior to planting can speed up germination). While parsley seedlings are readily available, they tend to dislike being transplanted and may or may not thrive, depending on the weather conditions. Monthly liquid feeds will keep plants growing well.

Growing in pots: a pot with a minimum top diameter of 20cm is recommended, and bigger is better.

Best time to sow: spring, summer and autumn. Raise plants from seed sown directly where they are to grow. Avoid transplanting at all times.

Picking tips: simply harvest leaves as required, and this picking can help keep plants bushy.

In the kitchen: after washing, flat-leaf parsley needs to be hung up to dry before chopping. Curly leaf parsley is far easier to wash then chop. This herb is best used fresh. Many cooks prefer to add freshly chopped parsley to a dish after it is cooked, just before serving.

Success secrets: mastering the art of raising plants from seed is the best way to grow parsley, although in many favourable climates parsley will happily 'self' seed, with new plants coming up to replace those which have lived out their lifespan.

Heaven with: many European sauces, including Italian pasta sauces, use parsley as a key ingredient, but parsley is also the basis of the Lebanese salad, tabouleh and Spanish salsa verde. Parsley marries well with fish, tomatoes, vegetables, lentils and rice, but its uses are many.

Parsley root: there is a third, less-well-known form of parsley, called Hamburg parsley (*Petroselinum tuberosum*) which is grown for its thick, parsnip-like root. Its flavour is a blend of parsley and celery, with a nutty quality. The foliage looks like flat-leaf parsley.

Risotto niçoise

Serves 4

3½ cups fish stock, heated, plus 2 tablespoons extra
500g/1lb fresh tuna steaks
1 teaspoon olive oil
4 cloves garlic, finely chopped
1 brown onion, chopped
2 cups Arborio rice
½ cup white wine
2 Pontiac potatoes, peeled and diced
200g/7oz green beans, trimmed
40g/1½oz parmesan cheese, grated
½ cup parsley, finely chopped
½ cup Kalamata olives, pitted

1 Heat ½ cup of the fish stock and add the tuna steaks. Poach gently for 5 minutes, then remove the fish from the liquid and dice. Reserve the cooking liquid.

2 Heat the olive oil and sauté the garlic and onion. Add the rice and stir to coat. Add the wine and allow liquid to be absorbed. Add the potatoes and mix.

3 Add 1 cup of stock and cook, stirring constantly, until liquid is absorbed. Add green beans, then continue adding remaining stock in the same way until it has all been used. Add the poaching liquid and stir well until absorbed. Remove the pan from the heat and add the extra stock and parmesan. Stir vigorously to combine, then garnish with parsley and olives. Serve immediately.

Pepper

Piper nigrum

There's more than one plant which produces a pepper-type spice for the kitchen. The greatest producer, in terms of worldwide true pepper production (excluding chillies which are not true peppers), is the tropical, evergreen climbing vine, *Piper nigrum*, which is native to the south-west Malabar coast of India but is now grown in many tropical countries (notably India, Indonesia Brazil, Malaysia and Vietnam). *P. nigrum* is the source of black pepper, white pepper and green peppercorns, which represent the same product in different stages of growth and processing. The *P. nigrum* vine grows up to 10m/33ft or more and bears clusters of 50 or more berries.

Black, white, green pepper: to produce black pepper, clusters are picked when not yet ripe then are left to dry in the sun until shrivelled and black. White pepper is made from fully ripened berries which are almost ready to turn red. After soaking in water to soften the outer coating, they are then sun-dried, during which time they are sun-bleached almost white. Green peppercorns are immature berries, which are preserved in brine.

Ground flavours: black pepper has the strongest, hottest flavour of the three. White pepper is milder, while green peppercorns are the mildest.

In the kitchen: all forms of pepper have their valuable uses, depending on the requirements of the dish, so it is worth stocking a range of them for use in cooking. White pepper, for example, is valuable in white or pale sauces where black pepper's flecks wouldn't be welcome. Teamed with salt, pepper is almost the universal seasoning in world cookery.

Chilli peppers: see Chillies listing, as these are often referred to as 'peppers' in the Americas.

Pepper trees: some members of the genus *Schinus* produce peppery berries, the most commonly encountered being pink peppercorns, which come from *S. terebinthifolius* and *S. molle*.

Sichuan pepper: this mainstay of Chinese cuisine is made from the dried fruits of *Zanthoxylum piperitum* and other species of *Zanthoxylum*, small trees native to eastern Asia. It is peppery in flavour, but its citrus tones make it a spice all on its own.

Native bush pepper: the Australian native pepperberry is harvested from *Tasmannia lanceolata*, native to eastern Australia.

Long pepper: from *Piper longum* and *P. retrofactum*, this is often used in Asian and African cookery and it looks like its name, 3–5cm/1.5–2in long dried catkins, which are usually used whole.

Sultana orange chicken

Serves 4

8 chicken drumsticks
½ cup lemon juice
1 small onion, finely chopped
zest of 1 large orange
1 teaspoon salt
freshly ground black pepper
½ teaspoon ground cinnamon
75g/2½oz ghee or butter
2–3 tablespoons sieved orange marmalade
 or apricot conserve
2 tablespoons coarsely crushed peppercorns
1 tablespoon dried mint

Orange Sultana Rice
1 cup medium-grain brown rice
1½ cups chicken stock
½ cup orange juice
grated zest of 1 orange
2–3 cups sultanas
¼ cup flaked or slivered toasted almonds
thin strips of orange zest

Curried Sultanas
3 tablespoons oil
1 teaspoon curry powder
¼ cup whole blanched almonds
1 cup sultanas

1 Combine lemon juice, onion, orange zest, salt, pepper and cinnamon and pour over chicken. Marinate in refrigerator for 1–2 hours, turning several times. Remove from marinade and pat dry.

2 Preheat oven to 180°C/350°F. Heat 3 tablespoons ghee in a pan and brown chicken lightly. Brush a baking dish with remaining ghee, then add drumsticks. Brush with marmalade then sprinkle with crushed peppercorns and mint. Bake for 45 minutes or until cooked, basting occasionally with ghee.

3 To make the orange sultana rice, combine rice with chicken stock, orange juice and zest. Bring to the boil, reduce heat to low, cover and cook for 15 minutes. Remove pan from the heat and allow to stand for 10 minutes. Stir through sultanas and almonds. Sprinkle with orange zest.

4 To make the curried sultanas, heat oil, add curry powder and cook 1 minute. Add almonds and toss over moderate heat for 2 minutes. Add sultanas and stir until plump.

5 Serve chicken with orange sultana rice and curried sultanas.

Perilla

Perilla frutescens

Widely used in Japan (where it is known as shiso), Korea and Vietnam (where it is called tia to), perilla is an aromatic herb related to mint and basil. Plants grow to 50–100cm/2.5–3.5ft tall, depending on the variety. The leaves, which might be all-green, all-red, or green on top and red underneath, have toothed edges, and the green leaves are smaller and have more pronounced toothed edges than the red leaves.

Growing basics: perilla is a sun-loving, warmth-loving, short-lived annual herb that does best in light soils in full sun or part shade. Germinating seeds can be erratic, but if all goes well seed comes up fairly quickly. When sowing, seeds should not be covered with soil, as they need light to germinate. Once established, perilla (especially the red variety) can then self-seed in the garden readily, to the point where it becomes a weed. Plants do not cope with frost, so in cooler climates they are grown in the warm season only, but in warm climates they will grow year-round. Growers pinch out the tops of plants to encourage more bushy growth.

Growing in pots: perilla can be grown in pots.

Picking tips: pick leaves as needed (you can keep them, in a plastic bag in the crisper section of your refrigerator for up to four days).

In the kitchen: perilla's aroma is warm and spicy, like mint but with a touch of anise (and green perilla is more aromatic than red). In Japanese cookery, shiso has many uses. Young green leaves are used in making sushi and sashimi, as wraps for rice cakes, and leaves are included in soups and salads. Both red and green leaves are battered and deep-fried, for tempura. Red perilla is also used as a food colouring, especially when pickling vegetables, fruits and ginger, and it is also used in making sweets. Perilla seeds are processed to produce an oil used in cooking, and the shoots of plants are also eaten or added to pickles.

In Vietnamese cuisine they shred the leaves and add them to soups and noodle dishes, but whole leaves also go into salads and as leafy wraps for rice and fish. In any cuisine perilla teams well with beef, chicken or fish, complements noodles, pasta, potatoes, tofu and rice, and blends in with other herbs such as basil, chives, lemon grass, parsley and wasabi.

Pomegranate

Punica granatum

Originally from the Middle-East and Northern India, the 4–5m/13–16ft tall pomegranate tree has much to offer both the garden and the kitchen. Highly ornamental, it produces big, showy orange flowers in late spring and a harvest of large, red fruit in autumn, plus an attractive autumn foliage colour display. It's the seeds (called arils) and juice of the fruit which have many uses in the kitchen.

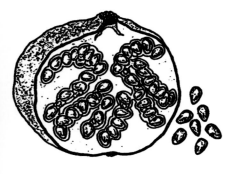

Growing basics: there are small-growing, purely ornamental forms of pomegranate tree with double-petalled flowers which produce no usable fruit. All double-flowering varieties do not produce useable fruit, whether tall-growing or not. The main thing is to buy the correct, larger-growing, productive tree from a fruit tree nursery. Plants are usually sold 'bare-rooted' in winter, when they are dormant, and that's the time to plant them into well-drained soil in a sunny spot. Pomegranates thrive in Mediterranean climates with a cool, wet winter and a hot, dry summer, but these are hardy trees which, once established, will grow well in many temperate areas, plus some subtropical zones. Though trees can form several trunks, many growers remove all but one, creating a single-trunked tree. Trees will also send up suckers (baby plants) around the base of the tree – these should be removed, as these can affect fruit production.

Growing in pots: pomegranate trees can be grown in very large pots.

Harvesting tips: autumn is harvest time for fruits, but don't be in a hurry to harvest them, as the longer fruits stay on the tree the sweeter they become. They should be picked when deep red, but before fruit starts to split. Fruits store well in a dry, cool place.

In the kitchen: it's the bright red arils and tangy juice which are used in cookery. Arils can be added whole to decorate and flavour salads, dips and desserts, and are a popular garnish. The juice, plus juice extracted from seeds, is used in Middle-Eastern cuisine to flavour sauces for meats and fish. Pomegranate molasses is sweet yet tart and is used in salad dressings, marinades and sauces. Dried seeds, called anardana, impart a sweet-sour taste to dishes, notably in Indian cuisines. Pomegranates are the flavour base for Grenadine liqueur.

Pomegranate tea: the juice of pomegranates adds a sweet-sour tang to teas, but it's not used to make tea on its own. Rich in vitamins A, C, E and iron, pomegranate juice contains folic acid and is high in anti-oxidants.

Pomegranate exotica

Serves 4

2 avocados
juice of ½ lime
2 papayas
60g/2oz mixed salad leaves
¾ cup pomegranate seeds
fresh cilantro/coriander to garnish

Dressing
1 mango
1 tablespoon rice wine vinegar
juice of 1 lime
½ teaspoon extra-virgin olive oil
1cm/0.5in piece ginger, peeled and finely chopped
½ teaspoon honey

1 Halve and peel the avocados, discarding the stones, then finely slice lengthwise. Gently toss in the lime juice in a large bowl.

2 Halve the papayas, then scoop out and discard the seeds. Peel and finely slice the flesh. Add to the avocado, then add the salad leaves and gently toss to combine.

3 To make the dressing, peel the mango, slice the flesh off the stone, then chop roughly. Blend to a thin purée with the vinegar, lime juice, oil, ginger and honey in a food processor.

4 Serve as individual side salads topped with the dressing and garnished with pomegranate seeds and cilantro leaves.

Poppy

Papaver somniferum

Commonly called 'poppyseed' by cooks, the seeds with so many uses in the kitchen come from the same plant from which opium is harvested – the oriental poppy, *Papaver somniferum*. In some countries the growing of this plant is illegal, so we'd advise you to be absolutely certain that it is permissible to grow Oriental poppies at home, before you start. The plant itself is a lovely summer-flowering annual, with light green leaves and large-petalled flowerheads in white, pink, red or purple colourings, sometimes marked by spots, on stalks 90cm/3ft tall.

Growing basics: Oriental poppies are native to South-East Europe, the Eastern Mediterranean and Central Asia, and will grow easily in temperate climates if you sow seed in spring, for flowering in summer and harvest in autumn. Grow plants in full sun in well-drained soil. Plants can be grown at other times in warmer climates (in frost-free zones seed can also be sown in autumn), but plants won't survive winter frosts. Seedlings are available in spring in nurseries, in countries which permit the growing of this plant. Please also note that if you don't collect the seed heads of this plant, it is very like to self-seed in your garden in subsequent years, so it is a potential weed.

Growing in pots: Oriental poppies can be grown successfully in pots.

Picking tips: allow flowers to finish and the large seed pods to develop fully. Wait until the pods turn yellowy-brown and feel dryish to the touch while still on the plant, then harvest and dry the pods completely in brown paper bags.

Open the pods with a knife to gather the many small seeds.

In the kitchen: poppyseeds can be either brown, grey-blue or white. Due to their high oil content, poppyseeds don't keep particularly well, going rancid over time, so it's best to buy small amounts and use them up fairly rapidly. Store them in an airtight jar, but freezing them is also a good storage option. Dry-roasting or baking poppyseeds will enhance their flavour, which is lightly nutty and sweet. Cooks and pastrychefs love to sprinkle poppyseeds over breads, breadrolls, cakes, bagels and pretzels. They're also used in fillings for strudels, sweet rolls and many other pastries. On the Indian subcontinent poppyseeds are used in curry pastes and, when ground, to thicken gravies. They complement a variety of vegetables, notably beans, cauliflower, potatoes and zucchinis/courgettes.

Lemon poppy cupcakes

Makes 12

2 eggs
125g/4oz butter, softened
1 cup caster sugar
½ cup Greek-style yoghurt
2 cups self-raising flour, sifted
zest of 2 lemons
juice of 1 lemon
1 teaspoon poppy seeds

Topping

1½ cups icing sugar
125g/4oz butter, softened
juice of 1 lemon
½ teaspoon poppyseeds
zest of 1 lemon
50g/1¾oz candied lemon, cut into thin slivers

1 Preheat the oven to 160°C/320°F. Line a 12-cupcake pan with cupcake papers. In a medium-sized bowl, lightly beat the eggs, add butter and sugar, then mix until light and fluffy.

2 Add yoghurt and flour, and stir to combine. Beat with an electric mixer for 2 minutes, until light and creamy. Stir through lemon zest, lemon juice and poppyseeds.

3 Divide the mixture evenly between the cake cases. Bake for 18–20 minutes until risen and firm to touch. Allow to cool for a few minutes and then transfer to a wire rack. Allow to cool fully before icing.

Topping

Combine all the topping ingredients except the candied lemon, mix and spoon onto cakes. Top with candied lemon pieces.

Pyrethrum

Tanacetum cinerariifolium

Gardeners who prefer to use a low-toxicity insect spray will probably be familiar with the pyrethrum-based products. The plant used to make the spray, *Tanacetum cinerariifolium*, is a member of the very large daisy family, Asteraceae. It produces solitary white daisy flowers with a yellow centre, atop slender stems and is native to the Balkan region in Central Europe but is now grown commercially in Europe, South Africa, Japan and other countries. The plant itself is a hardy little perennial about 30cm/1ft tall with grey-green leaves with a downy underside. The daisy flowers, which are harvested to make the insecticide, appear from early summer through to autumn.

Growing basics: pyrethrum can be grown by seed sown in spring, or by lifting, dividing and replanting established clumps in spring or autumn. It likes a well-drained soil and a sunny spot, but it copes very well with droughts and survives most winters. Over-fertilising is a common mistake, encouraging foliage growth but suppressing flower production.

Growing in pots: pyrethrum plants grow well in pots, but as with ground-grown plants, be sparing with fertilisers.

Picking tips: the flowerheads are harvested soon after they open, then dried. The insecticide product is made from the powdered, dried flowers.

In the kitchen: pyrethrum has no uses in the kitchen.

Home-made spray: to make your own pyrethrum spray, steep 30g/1oz of powdered pyrethrum flower in 30ml/1fl oz of methylated spirits, then dilute this in 14 litres /3 gallons of water. Spray this at dusk, as it decomposes in bright sunlight. Alternatively, instead of making a spray, just sprinkle the dried, powdered pyrethrum flowers around problem areas in the home or garden, to deter insects.

What about tansy? Pyrethrum has no uses in herbal medicine, although its close relative, tansy (*Tanacetum vulgare*) was used for centuries as a general health tonic. One thing tansy has in common with pyrethrum is that it, too, repels insects. However, the sad news is that tansy is toxic, rich in the chemical thujone (which is also present in wormwood, *Artemisia absinthium*). It's known to promote menstrual flow in women to such an extent that it poses a risk of aborting a foetus if taken internally. Other hazardous side-effects of taking too much include convulsions and psychotic reactions. Tansy is also an invasive weed in its growth habit, so remove flower heads before they form seeds.

Rice paddy herb

Limnophilia aromatica

Native to tropical regions of Asia, rice paddy herb is known as rau om and ngo om in Vietnam, the country which not only uses it most prolifically, but whose people have also introduced it to the rest of the world in the last 30 years. The plant itself is 15–30cm/6–12in tall, forms a low-growing mat in water, and grows wild throughout Vietnam and South-East Asia in ponds and, as its name implies, in flooded rice paddy fields. Its flowers are pinky-mauve, and its leaves and shoots have a citrussy aroma and a flavour of citrus blended with cumin.

Growing basics: rice paddy herb grows best in hot and humid tropical and subtropical climates in water, or on the edge of ponds, in full sun. In these areas it grows year-round. An easy way to get started is to strike some shop-bought herb in water (in shade), then grow this on in soil in a pond once it has formed roots. Some nurseries stock seedlings ready for planting.

Growing in pots: you can grow rice paddy herb in shallow potted water gardens. It's also grown as an aquarium plant, but not all aquarium plants have the correct flavour, as this plant species is very variable.

Picking tips: harvest leaves and stems as needed. The fresh young shoots and leaves are best.

In the kitchen: an essential ingredient in Vietnamese cooking, rice paddy herb is frequently chopped and added to soups just before serving. Many Vietnamese dishes, including the famous pho soups, are accompanied by a plate of herbs which can include mint, Vietnamese mint, bean sprouts, basil and rice paddy herb. In other South-East Asian countries, such as Thailand (where it is called phak khayang) it is often combined with the pungent fish/shrimp paste and chilli condiment called nam prik, to accompany curries; it is also used extensively in Cambodian cuisine (where it is called ma om) especially in fish dishes and in soups.

Best flavour partners for rice paddy herb are fish, seafood, all vegetables, coconut milk and noodles. It is often blended in with chilli, coriander, lemon grass, galangal and tamarind. If buying the herb from a shop, it will keep for about three days in a plastic bag in the crisper section of your refrigerator.

Rocket

Eruca vesicaria ssp. *sativa*

Known as arugula in Italy and rucola or roquette in other parts of Europe, this salad herb's English common name of rocket is appropriate, as it's a fast-growing small, leafy salad green less than 25cm/10in tall. Native to Asia and Southern Europe, 'cultivated' rocket (*Eruca vesicaria* ssp. *sativa*) is a short-lived annual with rounded leaves 2–3cm/1–1.5in wide. 'Wild' rocket (*Diplotaxis muralis*, and *D. erucoides*), a perennial native to the Mediterranean, belongs to another genus of plants, and has narrow, sharply toothed leaves on a plant up to 50cm/20in tall. Leaves of cultivated rocket have a nutty taste when young that turns into a more peppery bite later on. Wild rocket has a more peppery flavour even when young.

Growing basics: cultivated rocket is easy to grow and grows best from seed. In a sunny spot with well-drained soil, sow seeds and cover lightly with soil, water in with a light spray. In spring, summer and autumn seeds will germinate in less than a week, often just a few days. Water regularly and liquid feed monthly. Plants can bolt to seed in hot summer conditions, however. This rocket grows so quickly that you may need to sow several crops in the one growing season. Wild rocket, being perennial, grows on for a number of years and can be started from seed or seedlings.

Growing in pots: cultivated and wild rocket both grow easily in pots.

Picking tips: cultivated rocket tastes best when young, so start harvesting once plants are just 7–10cm/3–4in tall, and keep on harvesting regularly. Wild rocket can be picked at any time, but regular picking will produce more young, tender, less peppery new growth.

In the kitchen: rocket is used primarily as a salad green either on its own or as part of a salad of mixed greens. Older leaves, with their peppery bite, should be used sparingly in salads, although they can be cooked in stir-fries and other dishes requiring a leafy green vegetable. The classic flavour partners for rocket are olive oil, sharp cheeses such as parmesan or goat's cheese, and other herbs such as basil, parsley, coriander and mint.

Varieties: there are several different forms of rocket available. As well as the cultivated rocket and wild rocket, Turkish rocket (called rokka) is grown and used more as a vegetable than a salad green; and olive-leafed rocket is used as a salad green. Flavours vary from mild to pungent with different varieties.

Pictured left: wild rocket
Pictured right: cultivated rocket

Pork fillet with rocket, apple and parmesan salad

Serves 4

500g/1lb pork fillet

Salad
2 apples, thinly sliced
200g/7oz rocket, rinsed
shaved parmesan cheese
½ cup Italian dressing

Red wine and garlic marinade
½ cup red wine
¼ cup brown sugar
2 teaspoons crushed garlic
salt and pepper to taste

1 Heat all of the marinade ingredients in a pan, stir to combine, then allow to cool.

2 Trim the pork fillet of any sinew and fat, place in a shallow non-metallic dish. Pour over enough marinade to coat both sides. Cover and refrigerate for several hours or overnight.

3 Oil the grill bars and place on the apple slices. Cook until there are dark char lines and the apple is soft in texture.

4 Prepare the barbecue for direct heating. Oil the grill bars. Place on the marinated pork fillet and cook for 10 minutes each side, brushing with the extra marinade. Remove the pork and rest in a warm place while finishing preparing the salad.

5 In a large bowl place the rocket, grilled apples and a good handful of shaved parmesan.

6 Slice the pork fillet on the diagonal 1cm/0.5in thick and add to the salad. Divide the salad up onto four dinner plates and dress each salad with Italian dressing.

Rosemary

Rosmarinus officinalis

This classic Mediterranean perennial herb is *Rosmarinus officinalis*, a dense shrub with many thin, dark green, highly fragrant leaves. In gardens it now comes in several forms, including prostrate groundcovers. The typical colour of the small springtime flowers is blue, but pink- and white-flowered forms are readily available, too. As well as making an excellent addition to herb gardens, rosemary can make a very good hedge particularly in very dry areas, with plants spaced 1m apart.

Growing basics: rosemary needs good soil drainage and lots of sunshine to do well, but it dislikes high humidity and doesn't do so well in tropical and some subtropical areas. It also needs relatively little fertilising once established, so it can be an easy-care plant. Shrubby forms can reach between 60–150cm/2–5ft or taller. Prostrate forms grow well where they can spill down a masonry wall. Rosemary naturally grows in alkaline limestone soils, so in acid soil areas add lime or dolomite to raise the soil pH.

Growing in pots: a pot with a top diameter of at least 30cm/12in is recommended. Light applications of slow-release fertiliser in spring are all that's needed. Let soils dry out slightly between waterings. The prostrate groundcover forms will spill down the sides of pots, so a tall pot suits them best.

Best time to sow: rosemary is usually grown from cuttings or seedlings. Cuttings can strike very easily if taken in spring or autumn; in ideal circumstances cut pieces of stem will grow roots if planted straight into the soil. Spring, summer and autumn are all suitable planting times.

Picking tips: rosemary will grow much bushier if trimmed regularly, so trim more than you need each time you pick some.

In the kitchen: rosemary has a strong flavour, so the main tip is to use it sparingly in dishes.

Heaven with: potatoes, chicken, lamb, veal, rabbit, lemons, most vegetables, tomatoes, olive oil, garlic, lentils and other herbs such as bay, mint, oregano, parsley and thyme. It also makes a lovely topping for pizzas and a flavouring for savoury breads.

Barbecue skewers: The older stems of rosemary bushes can become quite stout, making them ideal as skewers for threading on meats and vegetables, kebab-style, at barbecues. Another good use for several stalks of rosemary is to strip off the top half of leaves, tie the bare ends together, then use the leafy other ends as a basting brush dipped in olive oil or a marinade. It's a terrific idea with barbecued lamb or chicken.

Roast potatoes with garlic and rosemary

Serves 8

1½kg/3lb chat potatoes
coarse sea salt
1 bulb garlic
6 sprigs rosemary, leaves removed and chopped
6 tablespoons olive oil

1 Preheat oven to 190°C/375°F. Place potatoes in a saucepan, cover with water, add salt and bring to the boil. Reduce heat and simmer for 2 minutes, then drain well. Make a few cuts across the tops of the potatoes. Break open the garlic and discard any loose pieces of skin.

2 Place potatoes and garlic cloves in a roasting dish, sprinkle with the chopped rosemary and oil. Bake for about 1¼ hours, turning occasionally, until crisp and golden brown. Transfer to a warmed serving dish, sprinkle with salt and garnish with extra rosemary sprigs.

Roses & rosehips

Rosa cvs.

After a rose flower finishes blooming it leaves behind a fruit called a rosehip, which in some varieties are harvested and used in making rosewater and dried rosehips. The varieties most used this way are the damask rose, *Rosa damascena*; the rugosa rose, *R. rugosa*; and the dog rose, *R. canina*. However, as fresh rose flower petals are also used in making tea, any variety of rose can be useful.

Growing basics: roses come in many forms and sizes, from groundcovers to bushes and shrubs through to climbing plants. Some flower once-only in spring, others flower repeatedly through spring, summer and autumn. All need full sunshine and regular feeding to grow well, most are dormant in winter, but once established these are hardy plants able to grow in a wide range of climates and soil types.

Growing in pots: roses can be grown in large pots.

Best time to plant: the traditional planting time for roses is midwinter, when they are dormant, but in frost-free temperate zones roses can be planted year-round.

Picking tips: pick individual flowers as needed, to harvest rose petals. Pick rosehips in autumn. *Note*: only roses not treated with chemical sprays should be used in the kitchen.

In the kitchen: it's in Middle-Eastern and Indian kitchens where rose flavourings abound, in the form of rosewater and dried rose buds. Most cooks buy ready-made rosewater, which is made from rosebuds which have been dried, then distilled. Rosewater has many uses in making sweets in Indian cookery (such as in gulab jamons, lassi yoghurt drinks, and kheer rice puddings). It's also the source of the red colouring in Turkish delight. Dried rose buds are usually ground and blended with other spices in Middle-Eastern, North African and Iranian cookery. Rose buds team well with spices such as cardamom, cinnamon, cloves, coriander, cumin, pepper, saffron and turmeric. Rose flavours complement fruits such as apples, apricots and quinces, and they go very well with rice, yoghurt, chestnuts and sweet desserts, and are turned into jams, jellies, syrups, wines and marmalades.

Rose tea: rosehips are high in Vitamin C; crush a few and pour over some boiling water to make a cup of tea. Fresh petals can also be turned into tea – use ¼ cup petals to 1 cup boiling water.

Rose oil: it's not the rose bush that provides the essential oil used in making rose oil fragrance – this most commonly comes from the rose-scented geranium.

Saffron

Crocus sativus

Long regarded as one of the world's most expensive spices by weight, due to the laborious hand-picking required, saffron has played the role of spice, dye and herbal remedy since ancient times. The plant from which it is produced is a flowering bulb (*Crocus sativus*) which is native to the Mediterranean, although no longer found in the wild. The main growing regions for saffron are Iran, Kashmir, Morocco and Spain, although it is now grown on a small scale in Tasmania and New Zealand.

Growing tips: the saffron crocus bulbs need a climate which experiences a very cold winter with many frosts, plus good winter rains and a hot, dry summer. The bulbs produce their leaves and mauve flowers in autumn. As so many flowers are needed for a very small supply, and its climatic needs are quite specialised, growing your own saffron crocus isn't practical.

Harvesting: saffron is the plant's yellow-orange pollen, often called 'threads' or 'filaments'. It is laboriously collected by removing the style and stigmas from each flower by hand. When you consider that around 160 flowers need to be harvested to get just one gram of saffron, it's easy to see why the product is so expensive.

In the kitchen: saffron is often soaked in hot water for a few minutes, prior to being used in cooking; this saffron liquid is then added to the dish. While saffron has many uses in cooking, it is most popularly associated with rice dishes, bringing a wonderful yellow colour to the rice, along with saffron's musky, floral scent.

It's commonly added to soups and stews, cakes and breads, and it teams well with many other spices, including anise, cardamom, cinnamon, fennel, ginger, nutmeg, pepper and paprika. As saffron is very expensive, use it sparingly. Saffron threads keep their flavour for two to three years if stored in an airtight container in a cupboard.

Saffron tea: saffron is either consumed as a tea on its own, or as a way of colouring and flavouring green tea. Very little saffron is needed to make tea, as it has a powerful colouring and flavour.

Cheap substitutes: turmeric is often used in some inferior 'saffron powder' products, so too cheap food dyes. Even cheap quality saffron is sometimes artificially dyed (soaked in water it changes the water colour quickly). Good quality saffron takes a few minutes to change the colour of its soaking water.

Delicious bouillabaisse

Serves 6

3kg/6lb mixed fish and seafood, including firm white
    fish fillets, prawns/shrimp, mussels, crab and
    calamari rings
¼ cup olive oil
2 cloves garlic, crushed
2 large onions, chopped
2 leeks, sliced
2 x 400g/28oz canned tomatoes
150g/5 oz fish stock
1 tablespoon chopped fresh thyme or
    1 teaspoon dried thyme
2 tablespoons chopped fresh basil or
    1½ teaspoons dried basil
2 tablespoons chopped fresh parsley
2 bay leaves
2 tablespoons finely grated orange rind
1 teaspoon saffron threads
150g/5 oz dry white wine
freshly ground black pepper

1 Remove the bones and skin from the fish fillets and cut into 2cm/¾in cubes. Peel and devein the prawns, leaving the tails intact. Scrub and remove the beards from the mussels. Cut the crab into quarters. Set aside.

2 Heat a slow cooker on a high setting, then add the oil, garlic, onions, leeks, tomatoes and stock and cook for 1½ hours. Add the thyme, basil, parsley, bay leaves, orange rind, saffron and wine. Cook for 30 minutes.

3 Add the fish and crab and cook for 1 hour. Add the remaining seafood and cook for 1 hour longer or until all fish and seafood are cooked. Season to taste with black pepper.

Sage

Salvia officinalis

The genus *Salvia* has around 750 species, including many culinary herbs, but there are also many pretty flowering forms of sage which are not used as herbs in the kitchen at all, so be careful which sage plant you choose to bring home to your herb garden. The plant called common sage, *Salvia officinalis*, is an excellent choice for herb gardens, as it's a spreading low shrub with grey-green leaves and purple-blue flowers. It's up to 90cm/3ft high and 75cm/30in wide.

Growing basics: sage loves lots of sunshine, needs well-drained soil but doesn't like excessively rich soil nor humidity in summer. For that reason sage doesn't do well in the humid tropics and subtropics, but it thrives in cool and temperate zones, especially those with dry summers.

Growing in pots: only one sage plant is needed per pot, which should be at least 30cm/12in across at the top. Sit the pot on pot feet to ensure good soil drainage, feed lightly in spring with a slow-release fertiliser and let the potting mix dry slightly between waterings.

Best time to sow: as you will need only one sage plant, it's best to start from a single seedling, although sage can be grown from seed. Spring is the ideal planting time in cool zones, but in warmer temperate areas it can be planted at any time of year.

Picking tips: sage is a strongly flavoured herb so you won't need much for most dishes. The young green leaves are not as strongly flavoured as the older grey leaves.

In the kitchen: sage leaves don't keep well so just pick leaves as you need them. One way to use sage is via sage butter—start cooking by melting butter in a pan, fry sage leaves to flavour the butter, then add the other ingredients for that dish.

Success secrets: prune back sage plants all over, by up to one-third of its size, after flowering finishes in spring. The flush of new growth will look most appealing later on.

Heaven with: veal, chicken, pork, goose and duck. Sage and onion stuffing is the classic choice for Thanksgiving turkeys in the United States.

Varieties: many! Very popular choices for herb gardens include purple-leafed sage (rarely flowers, has a milder flavour), variegated golden sage (which rarely flowers), pineapple sage (with longer leaves and red flowers), and clary sage (shorter lived, large leaves, large ornamental flower heads). Greek sage is strongly flavoured with large grey-green leaves; use it sparingly.

Pork and sage-filled ravioli

Serves 4

24 wonton skins
1 egg yolk, beaten with 1 tablespoon water
40g/1½oz parmesan cheese, grated

Pork and Sage Filling
300g/10½oz ricotta cheese, drained
150g/5oz lean cooked pork, diced
60g/2oz lean bacon, finely chopped
40g/1½oz parmesan cheese, grated
¼ cup fresh parsley, chopped
¼ cup fresh sage, chopped
ground nutmeg
freshly ground black pepper

Sage and Butter Sauce
125g/4oz butter
¼ cup sage, chopped

1 To make filling, place ricotta, pork, bacon, parmesan, parsley, sage, nutmeg and black pepper in a bowl and mix to combine.

2 Lay 12 wonton skins on bench. Place a teaspoon of filling in the centre of each one, brush edges with egg yolk mixture and place the remaining wonton skins on top. Press edges together.

3 Cook ravioli, a few at a time, in boiling water for 4 minutes or until tender. Drain and sprinkle with parmesan cheese.

4 In a saucepan melt the butter and add the chopped sage, cook for 2 minutes. Pour over the ravioli to serve.

Salad herbs

Our book of herbs and spices is filled with herbs which can be added to salads. In addition to all these, there are numerous other salad herbs well worth growing in gardens that can give your mixed leaf salads extra flavour, colour and individuality.

Growing tips: most salad herbs can be grown together, as they generally like the same growing conditions of fertile, well-drained soil and lots of sunshine. Plants can be grown from seed or seedlings sown in spring and summer in cool temperate climates, but in warmer climates they can be planted year-round. However, many will bolt to flower and seed rapidly in very hot weather, and hot climates generally. In these hot conditions, some midday or afternoon shade is advisable, as is good watering. Fortnightly liquid fertilising will promote better growth, and as a general rule, the faster plants grow the more tender and flavoursome the leaves, and the slower they grow, the more bitter the leaves.

Growing in pots: salad herbs are perfectly suited to growing in pots; generally a pot that is much wider than it is deep is the best shape, as these plants' roots do not go deep but plants do need room to spread.

Harvesting tips: if harvesting just a few leaves, take these from the outside of the plant. Otherwise, plants can be harvested whole, if preferred. Younger leaves are generally more tender than older leaves.

In the kitchen: washing and drying leaves before adding to salads is an essential step.

Lettuce: *Lactuca sativa*, or lettuce, are divided into two basic types: heart-forming lettuce such as 'Iceberg', 'Butter', 'Mignonette' and 'Cos' all with a central cluster of leaves; and open-hearted or loose-leaf lettuce such as 'Oakleaf', which do not form hearts. The heart-forming lettuce are usually harvested whole, while the outer leaves of open-hearted lettuce are harvested repeatedly. The number of lettuce varieties is enormous, offering a choice of leaf colours and textures.

Corn salad: *Valerianella locusta* is a low-growing salad herb with rosettes of small, rounded leaves. Also called lamb's lettuce or, in France, mâche, it is valued for its pleasant, nutty flavour.

Mesclun: this is not so much a plant on its own but a grouping of salad plants grown from seed to create a 'mixed leaf' salad when harvested. While the contents of mesclun seed mixes vary, you will often find rocket, corn salad, endive, lettuce, mustard, beet and sorrel included.

Pictured left: radicchio

Savory

Satureja spp.

There are several edible forms of the fragrant herb *Satureja*, but the two most common ones used in kitchens are summer savory (*S. hortensis*) and winter savory (*S. montana*); both are native to southern Europe and the Mediterranean. Summer savory is an annual plant 30cm/12in tall with soft grey leaves and white or pink flowers in summer. Winter savory is a small 30cm/12in tall perennial shrub with tougher, dark green leaves and lavender or white flowers in summer. Being an annual, summer savory dies once winter arrives, but perennial winter savory lives on through the cold months.

Growing basics: summer savory grows quickly from very fine seed sown in a sunny spot in spring. Winter savory can be grown from seed sown in spring, but it can also be grown from divisions taken from an existing plant in spring. Both types of savory need well-drained soils to grow well, but extra fertiliser is unnecessary. Temperate climates suit both plants best.

Growing in pots: both plants can be grown successfully in pots.

Picking tips: pick leaves as needed, and regular picking of summer savory in particular will encourage more bushy, younger growth on plants, which produces better leaves for the kitchen.

In the kitchen: slow-cooked dishes suit the pungent flavour of savory well, but the general rule with these herbs is not to use too much. Summer savory has hints of thyme, mint and marjoram; winter savory has a stronger flavour, more resembling another strong herb, sage. Summer savory goes well with many vegetables, notably dishes containing beans and other legumes (its other common name is bean herb). It also combines well with cabbage and root vegetables. Winter savory will add flavour to slow-cooked lamb, pork and game dishes, and those containing oily fish such as salmon and mackerel. Rather than using either type of savory on its own, many cooks combine it with other herbs such as basil, bay, lavender, marjoram, mint, oregano, parsley, rosemary or thyme. Both herbs are also well suited to flavouring vinegars.

Medicinal benefits: summer savory is a useful medicinal herb. Research shows that it is good for digestive disorders, a carminative that suppresses gas in the intestines, an appetite stimulant and it can also help to lessen diarrhoea, says *Tyler's Honest Herbal*. Unfortunately, Tyler also says there's no evidence to support the traditional belief that winter savory is an aphrodisiac.

Pictured left: summer savory
Pictured right: winter savory

Scented geraniums

Pelargonium spp.

Though there is a genus of plants called *Geranium*, the plants which botanists call *Pelargonium* are known to gardeners worldwide as geraniums. Most are native to Southern Africa, and fragrances range from apple to lemon, mint, nutmeg, rose, stunning peppermint and many others. As the *Pelargonium* genus has around 230 members, and numerous hybrids, there are many plant sizes, leaf colours and shapes, and flower colours to choose from. Within this big group, the scented-leaf pelargoniums are valued for their fragrant foliage rather than their flowers, which tend to be small if still quite pretty. Most popular among gardeners are lemon-scented geranium (*P. crispum*) and rose-scented geranium (*P. graveolens*).

Growing basics: scented geraniums grow best from cuttings taken in late spring, summer or early autumn, as they form new roots easily from cuttings. These plants need very good soil drainage and generally prefer drier climates; they dislike prolonged humidity in summer (which can cause fungal diseases), and won't survive winter frosts. They'll grow in positions ranging from full sun to partial shade (the popular lemon-scented geranium copes well with partial shade).

Growing in pots: they're well suited to growing in pots, and in areas with frosty winters, pots (which can be brought under shelter) are the only way to grow them.

Harvesting: plants are cut down in late summer for processing to distill their essential oils.

In the kitchen: though edible, scented geranium leaves have a strong flavour that needs to be used judiciously. The pretty little flowers make a nice edible garnish for salads. Some cooks scent a jar of caster sugar, for making desserts, by adding just a few rose geranium leaves to the jar and leaving it for two weeks. Other cooks line the base of cake tins with rose-scented geranium to flavour sponge cakes. It's rose-scented geranium which has the greatest uses in the kitchen, notably in flavouring sweet dishes and desserts.

Rose-scented geranium tea: to make a cup of tea, steep 3 rose-scented geranium leaves in 1 cup of boiling water for 5 minutes, then strain. Though the scientific evidence for its health benefits is lacking, its advocates say this is a soothing tea which relieves headaches and anxiety.

Rose oil: did you know the most commonly available rose-scented essential oil comes from the rose-scented geranium, and not roses themselves?

Sesame

Sesamum orientale

This annual plant has been grown for its oil-rich seeds since the times of the Ancient Egyptians and Babylonians, thousands of years ago, and sesame products are still as valuable as ever, from Europe to the Middle-East and across to South-East Asia, Japan, Korea and China. The sesame plant itself (*S. orientale* syn. *S. indicum*) is not often grown in domestic gardens, but is widely grown in tropical countries, notably India and Burma. It's an annual tropical plant 50–100cm/20–40in tall, with 5cm/2in long leaves and tubular flowers in either white, blue or purple. Following the flowers are the 2–8cm/1–3in long seed capsules. Seeds produced are oval, shiny and flat, varying in colour from creamy white to pale yellow, red, brown or black.

Growing basics: as sesame is a tropical annual it grows best in those climates and so isn't suited to home cultivation in temperate zones. In subtropical zones it may be grown at home. Sesame plants produce an extensive root system and so are very drought-tolerant.

Growing in pots: sesame is not well suited to growing in pots.

Picking tips: processing and drying harvested seed pods is not an easy task for the home gardener, as moisture levels in the pods must be keep very low at all times, so it's not recommended to try this at home.

In the kitchen: both sesame oil and sesame seeds have countless uses in many cuisines. Dark amber Asian sesame oil is made from dry-roasted seeds and, due to its low burn temperature, it is mostly used in marinades, sauces and dressings in Japanese, Korean and Chinese cooking. A lighter coloured sesame oil is used in Indian and Burmese cookery, and a Burmese curry wouldn't be authentic without the basic ingredients first being cooked slowly in light sesame oil. In the Middle-East, sesame seeds are sprinkled onto breads before baking; the paste made from sesame, called tahini, is used to make the chickpea dip, hummus; and sesame seeds are the basis of the sweet treat, halva. White sesame seeds are teamed with soy sauce and sugar in Japan to make dressings for a variety of salads. Black seeds are used in Chinese cookery to coat fish and seafood prior to cooking. Generally, sesame seeds complement many vegetables and legumes. Sesame's flavour teams well with spices such as cardamom, cinnamon, cloves, ginger, nutmeg, oregano, pepper and thyme. Sesame seeds should be stored in an airtight container in the cupboard.

Asian greens with sweet soy and sesame dressing

Serves 4

500g/1lb baby bok choy
500g/1lb Chinese broccoli
285g/10oz water spinach
½ teaspoon sesame oil
1 tablespoon oyster sauce
1 tablespoon kecap manis
1 tablespoon rice vinegar
1 tablespoon sesame seeds, toasted

1 Cut the bok choy, Chinese broccoli and water spinach into 20cm/8in lengths. Wash, drain and put in a large bamboo steamer lined with baking paper. Cook over a wok of simmering water, making sure the base of the steamer does not come in contact with the water, for 5 minutes or until vegetables are bright green and tender.

2 Whisk together the sesame oil, oyster sauce, kecap manis and rice vinegar in a jug.

3 Neatly pile the vegetables onto a serving plate and drizzle with the sauce. Sprinkle with sesame seeds and serve.

Sichuan pepper

Zanthoxylum simulans

The province of Sichuan (also spelled Szechwan) in China is famous for its spicy cuisine, as the pepper named after the province is the dried fruits of a prickly ash tree, *Zanthoxylum simulans*. This is not related to the plant which produces black, white and green pepper, *Piper nigrum* (see page 200 for more on pepper). The prickly ash tree is a small deciduous tree or shrub 2–6m/6–20ft tall that's native to western China generally. Its greenish flowers are produced in midsummer, and these are followed by red berries in autumn, which are harvested and dried to make Sichuan pepper. To produce berries, both male and female plants are needed.

Growing basics: as you'll need both a male and female plant to produce berries, this isn't a tree that is much grown in gardens, nor is it readily available. Growing best in cool temperate climates in positions ranging from full-sun to part shade, it copes with a variety of soil types, as long as they are well-drained.

Harvesting: the berries are harvested in autumn, then sun-dried until they become reddish-brown and split open. The bitter and gritty inner black seeds are discarded.

In the kitchen: for authentic Sichuan cuisine, no substitute for Sichuan pepper is acceptable. Its flavour is more peppery than black pepper, is fragrant with a woody aroma with hints of citrus, and taste-testing it will leave a numbing effect on your tongue. It's available either as whole, split berries or crushed berries blended with salt. With the split berries, check them for the presence of black seeds and discard any that you find. Before crushing split berries, dry-roast them to bring out the flavour and make it easier to crush the berries. Sichuan pepper is one of the five spices used to make Chinese five-spice powder, which is used extensively in Chinese cuisine. Used on its own, Sichuan pepper is used to flavour roasted, grilled or fried meats and poultry (eg, crisp skin chicken), and it's added to vegetable stir-fries and soups. Air-tight containers are the best way to store Sichuan pepper, but the split berries will last longer than the powder. Sichuan pepper oil is also available from specialty Chinese grocery shops.

Japanese sansho: in Japan, a closely related tree, *Z. piperitum*, produces a similar, dried peppery berry called sansho, usually sold as a coarse crushed powder.

Sichuan beef stir-fry

Serves 4

600g/21oz beef tenderloin, thinly sliced
1½ teaspoons Sichuan pepper
2 bunches gai lan (Chinese broccoli), cut into
   5cm/2in lengths
½ cup char siu sauce

1 Preheat a large non-stick frying pan or wok on high heat.

2 Place the beef and Sichuan pepper in a medium bowl and stir to combine. Add the beef to the pan and cook, stirring occasionally, for 1–2 minutes or until browned. Add the gai lan and cook for a further 2 minutes. Pour in the char siu sauce, heat through and toss to combine.

3 Divide the beef stir-fry evenly amongst four serving bowls.

Note Char siu sauce is a specialty barbecue sauce made with soy sauce, honey, sugar, dry sherry, salt, Chinese five-spice powder and crushed fresh ginger.

Sorrel

Rumex spp.

Two species of sorrel are grown in gardens, French sorrel (*Rumex scutatus*) and garden sorrel (*R. acetosa*), and both are naturally widespread throughout Europe and western Asia. Of the two, garden sorrel is more commonly grown and is a larger plant (60-100cm/2–3ft), but French sorrel (20–50cm/18–30in tall), with its lighter, lemony flavour is well worth planting, too. Both are spreading perennials with mid-green, spinach-like leaves. Sorrel is mostly considered to be a salad green, but with its sour taste it can also be used as a herb and to make sorrel soup.

Growing basics: sorrel can be grown across a wide range of climates, from cool temperate through to the subtropics (although in hotter climates it will need afternoon shade and good watering). It grows easily from seed sown in spring, but as it's a perennial it can be started by dividing and replanting an existing clump in autumn or spring. In temperate climates it needs a sunny spot (but some shade is OK) and well-drained, fertile soil, plus regular watering. The main job is to remove all flowers to prevent the setting of seed. If plants are ignored and seed is set, the leaves will become too bitter and new sorrel plants will spring up everywhere – it is a potential weed. In frost-free, warm climates sorrel will stay green all through winter.

Growing in pots: sorrel can be grown successfully in pots, and it is also worth growing indoors in a sunny area.

Picking tips: you can harvest the leaves once plants are 10cm/4in tall, and keep on harvesting leaves regularly to keep plants compact.

If leaves become big and bitter, cut down plants almost to the ground, give them a liquid feed and they will regrow a new crop of tender leaves.

In the kitchen: sorrel is high in oxalic acid and so eating too much can have unpleasant side-effects, so the main thing with it is never to use too much, and it is not used as a dish on its own. Its lemony flavour, however, is very pleasant in small amounts in salads, and it is often used in tandem with spinach. Sorrel combines very well with chervil, chives, dill, parsley, rocket, savory, spring onions, tarragon and thyme. In traditional European cookery you'll find sorrel in soups, egg dishes such as omelettes, in potato salads and as a garnish to accompany oily fish such as salmon, trout or sardines.

Sorrel soup

Serves 6–8

50g/1¾oz butter
1 medium-sized onion, finely diced
1 stalk celery, thinly sliced
1 leek, white part only, thinly sliced
1 small carrot, washed and diced
1 tablespoon finely chopped parsley
salt and pepper to taste
1kg/36oz fresh sorrel
1.5 litres/2.5 pints good beef or chicken stock
sour cream for serving

1 Heat butter in a frying pan, add onions and gently fry until transparent, stirring occasionally. Add the prepared celery, leek, carrot and parsley and cook while stirring for 4 minutes. Season with salt and pepper; set aside.

2 Trim off the thicker lower part of the stem of the sorrel and wash well. With water still clinging to leaves place in a large saucepan. Pour in 1 cup boiling water, cover and boil slowly for 6–8 minutes. Cool slightly then puree in a blender or food processor with the liquid.

3 Pour the beef or chicken stock into the large saucepan, add the fried vegetables and sorrel puree and cover and simmer for 20 minutes. Adjust seasoning.

4 Serve in soup bowls. Pass a bowl of sour cream around to add at will.

St John's wort

Hypericum perforatum

Native to Europe and Western Asia, where it has been valued in herbal medicine since the time of the Ancient Greeks, St John's wort gets its name from the fact that it is in flower in Europe on St John the Baptist's Day, 24 June. The name 'wort' is an old Anglo-Saxon word meaning medicinal herb. When growing your own, obtain the correct plant, *Hypericum perforatum*, as there are several related plants, also called St John's wort, but which don't have the medicinal benefits of *H. perforatum*. This is an aromatic perennial 30–90cm/1–3ft tall with scented yellow to golden flowers in summer, whose petals wear tiny black dots around the edges. Its leaves are small, pale green, stalkless and have tiny perforations (hence the species name, *perforatum*).

Growing basics: you can grow St John's wort from seed sown in spring, or you can lift, divide and replant divisions of established plants in autumn or spring. It prefers well-drained soil in either full sun or partial shade. Fertilise sparingly but water regularly. It's best to cut off flowers before they set seed, as this plant can readily self-seed and become weedy.

Growing in pots: it needs a large pot, regular watering and very light feeding.

Picking tips: harvest the flowers and a few leaves as needed, during summer.

Medicinal benefits: the popularity of St John's wort in recent decades has seen it studied intensively, and research does back up the claims that it is an effective anti-depressant and has anti-inflammatory properties. However, it has also been shown that excessive use has serious side-effects, most notably a sensitivity to light and sunshine that can lead to skin disorders (dermatitis) and inflammation of the mucous membranes. It's strongly advised to consult a doctor before using St John's wort.

Making tea: use mostly fresh flowering tops plus a few leaves to make tea, pouring 1 cup boiling water over ¼ cup of flowers and leaves. Let it steep for 5 minutes. Sweeten with honey to taste. Remember, please be cautious in your use of it. Limit your intake of tea to just one cup per day, and drink this tea for no more than 10 days in a row. After that, take a week off from drinking it.

Star anise

Illicium verum

Also known as Chinese star anise, this spice has a warm, spicy fragrance and aniseed flavour that is very refreshing. Its name comes from the eight-pointed star shape of its dried seed pods. Following the creamy white flowers which turn pink or purple in summer, the seed pods are harvested in autumn. The plant itself (*Illicium verum*) is a small, evergreen tree native to China and Vietnam but now grown throughout South and South-East Asia. Trees don't bear fruit until about six years old, but are long-lived, up to 100 years. The active ingredient in star anise is anethole, the same substance found in the unrelated but similar tasting spice, anise (*Pimpinella anisum*).

Growing tips: star anise will grow in temperate, subtropical and tropical climates. In cultivation, most star anise trees are kept down to 3–5m/10–18ft tall plants, but in the wild they can get much bigger, up to 18m/60ft. These trees grow best in semi-shade or dappled sunlight in moist, well-drained acidic soil. Water regularly and mulch around the tree to preserve soil moisture.

Harvesting: picked while still green, the seed pods are then dried in the sun, at which point they turn reddy-brown and become fragrant.

In the kitchen: star anise is used either as whole pods or as a ground powder (the ground product is a mix of seeds and dried fruit). Whole pods are often added to flavour soups and stocks, while the ground product is one of the five ingredients in the Chinese five-spice powder (along with cloves, cinnamon, Sichuan pepper and fennel). Star anise has countless uses in Asian cuisine, teaming very well with duck, chicken and pork dishes, as well as many vegetables. Many sweet Chinese dessert dishes use ground star anise. In European cookery, whole star anise is added to poaching liquids for cooking fruits including stone fruits, quinces, apples and pears. It also complements leeks, pumpkin, sweet potato and potato dishes. Star anise marries well with chicken, fish, seafood and pork. It combines well with a variety of spices, including cinnamon, fennel, coriander, chilli, Sichuan pepper, ginger and lemon, so it's found in many spice blends as well. Whole pods will keep for about one year in an airtight container in a cupboard.

Star anise tea: both spicy Thai tea and Indian chai tea make good use of star anise.

Sumac

Rhus coriaria

Providing a tart yet fruity flavour, dried crushed sumac berries are a key ingredient in Lebanese cookery and Arabic cooking generally. Its flavour plays the same role as lemon juice in cookery. The plant itself, commonly called elm-leafed sumach, is an attractive, bushy shrub 3m/10ft tall that is native to elevated parts of the Mediterranean, notably Sicily, Lebanon and Turkey, plus Iran. Its colourful autumn foliage display is very attractive, and at this time of year, its white flowers develop into clusters of small, round, rust-coloured berries.

Growing basics: there's one very good reason not to grow sumac at home, and that's the fact that, being a species of *Rhus*, it can cause severe allergic reactions in some people who come in contact with its foliage or berries. (However, there appear to be no allergy problems with people consuming the dried, prepared spice, sumac, made from the plant's berries.) Generally, though, the plant grows in poor, rocky soils in very cool to cold areas with wet winters and dry summers.

Growing in pots: due to its allergy-causing properties, it's not worth growing in pots at home.

Harvesting: berries are picked in autumn when not quite fully ripe, then sun-dried and crushed.

In the kitchen: few Middle-Eastern cooks would grow and process their own sumac, instead buying commercially grown and crushed sumac at the local market or shop. Sumac comes either as a very fine, red-brown powder, or as a more coarsely ground product, or sometimes as whole, dried berries which are crushed at home. The classic Middle-Eastern spice mix of za'atar combines sumac berries, sesame seeds and crushed dried thyme (usually a thyme variety called za'atar). The role of sumac in Middle-Eastern cuisine is similar to that of salt – ie, it brings out the flavour in the other ingredients. Sumac powder is rubbed onto meats and fish before cooking, it's sprinkled onto breads before baking, it's also added to salads such as fattoush, and sprinkled simply over sliced raw onion as a side dish. Sumac berries are cracked and soaked in water for half an hour, and the resulting tart liquid is used in marinades, salad dressings and sometimes also blended into drinks. You can also add sumac to casseroles and soups. It combines well with many spices, including chilli, coriander, cumin, mint, paprika and sesame. Sumac keeps very well in airtight containers.

Grilled sumac fish

Serves 4

4 white-fleshed fish fillets
  (500–600g/17½oz–21oz each)
4 tablespoons olive oil
2 tablespoons sumac
bunch of fresh dill
2 lemons, sliced
4 serves of mixed Mediterranean vegetables
8–12 bamboo skewers, soaked in water for 30 minutes

1 Ask the fishmonger to clean and gut the fish and remove the head. Cut off the fins and trim the tail with a pair of kitchen scissors. In a small bowl mix together the olive oil and the Sumac. Wash the dill and trim off the stalks.

2 Place the fish on their backs on a chopping board. Into each fish cavity place a good handful of dill and 2–3 slices of lemon, then pour on some of the oil and sumac. With 2–3 small wooden skewers, fasten together the fish so dill and lemon do not fall out during cooking.

3 Turn the fish over and rub the oil and sumac well into the fish.

4 Prepare the barbecue for direct-heat cooking. Oil the grill bars well. Cook the fish on each side for 8–10 minutes. To serve, place the mixed Mediterranean vegetables onto a plate and place the flathead on top.

Sunflower

Helianthus annuus

Native to the Americas, sunflowers come in a huge array of forms and sizes. Some are single-stemmed, others are multi-branched, several are spectacularly tall, over 3m/10ft, others have huge flower heads up to 25cm/10in across, and there are 1m/3ft dwarf forms. Most are fast-growing annuals which produce yellow daisy flowers in summer. The main thing with growing sunflowers for their seeds is to plant the right variety: some seeds (which are all-black) are only for oil production; other seeds (which are black with white stripes) are for eating, and there are many which are purely ornamental, too small to be harvested easily and eaten. The best varieties for eating are those which are taller-growing and produce large, black and white seeds, such as 'Mammoth Russian', 'Russian Giant', 'Kong', 'Giganteus', 'Grey Stripe', 'Jumbo' and 'Paul Bunyan Hybrid'.

Growing basics: sunflowers are best grown from seeds planted where they are to grow, in full-sun in well-drained, fertile soil in spring in temperate and cool climates. In subtropical and tropical zones, sow seeds in spring, summer and autumn. Taller-growing varieties will need to be sheltered from winds, or staked.

Growing in pots: dwarf varieties are ideal for growing in pots outdoors, but won't produce edible seeds.

Picking tips: sunflower seeds develop in autumn. Harvest seeds by cutting off the flower heads once flowers start to turn brown; place these in a bag and hang up until fully dry. You can also let seeds dry on the plant as it wilts and dies off, placing a bag over the flower head to catch the seeds as they fall. Fresh flower petals can also be harvested as needed in summer, for use as a garnish in garden salads.

In the kitchen: sunflower seeds are eaten either raw or roasted as a snack food. Seeds can be sprouted and the sprouts added to salads and sandwiches. Seeds are added to soups, stir-fries, rice dishes and sauces either as whole seeds or as a ground powder. They're also added to cakes, puddings and biscuits, and are a good source of iron, zinc and Vitamin C.

Kid friendly: with their easy-to-handle, large seeds, rapid growth and cheery flowers, these are an ideal first plant for children to grow.

Bird friendly: eating sunflower seeds is not easy, as each seed needs to be cracked to remove the husk, so the best reason to grow edible sunflower seeds is to feed them to your pet birds, who'll love them.

Tamarind

Tamarindus indica

A widely cultivated tree of the tropics, the tamarind tree is valued not only for its sweet and sour fruit pods, but also because it's a superb, long-lived shade tree. Though originally from East Africa, its botanical name of *Tamarindus indica* reflects the misconception that it's native to India, where it has been grown for thousands of years. The tropical zones of all continents have many old, established tamarind trees in towns, parks, gardens and plantations.

Growing tips: tamarind trees are large (up to 24m/80ft tall) and slow-growing, producing a wide, shady canopy. Not fussy about the soil in which it grows, it can also grow close to the seaside. Once established the fruiting is prolific, with harvests of 150kg/330lb per tree common. Tamarind trees do produce pale yellow flowers, but these are small. It's the large (5–15cm/2–6in long) rust-coloured seed pods which are the prize. However, the young leaves are also used in Indian and South-East Asian cooking.

Harvest: the unripe pods have green flesh and are too sour, so growers wait until the sticky flesh inside turns a reddy-brown colour.

In the kitchen: with its sweet yet sour flavour, tamarind lends itself to a huge array of both savoury and sweet dishes, plus condiments, sauces, chutneys, jams, pickles and drinks. It's a key ingredient in cuisines of regions as varied as South-East Asia, India, the Caribbean and Mexico.

Preparing tamarind: whole tamarind pods are readily available in the tropics. The pods are brittle and open easily; the sticky pulp inside is then soaked in water to remove the seeds, then the mixture of water and pulp is used in cooking. Outside the tropics you're more likely to find the pulp either compressed into a block (which is also soaked), or a processed concentrate packed into jars. Both of these products have a long shelf life. One common way to use tamarind is to prepare tamarind water (it's comparable to lemon or lime juice). To make tamarind water, soak 40g/1.5oz of tamarind pulp in ½ cup hot water. Stir then leave it for 30 minutes. Strain the liquid and discard the pulp.

Tamarind tea: yes, tamarind can be turned into a sweet-sour tea to which you may need to add some sugar to get the flavour balance right. Tamarind is a rich source of Vitamin C, potassium, calcium, phosphorus, iron and magnesium. It also contains carotenes and is high in anti-oxidants.

Crispy fried duck

Serves 4

2 tablespoons soy sauce
1 tablespoon tamarind paste
1cm/0.5in piece fresh ginger, grated
1 clove garlic, crushed
1 teaspoon ground coriander
¼ cup peanut oil
4 duck breasts

1 Combine soy sauce, tamarind paste, ginger, garlic, coriander and 1 tablespoon of the oil to make a marinade. Pour marinade over duck and leave to marinate in the refrigerator for 2–3 hours.

2 Preheat oven to 200°C/400°F. Heat remaining oil in a frying pan. Add duck and cook for 1–2 minutes or until golden and crisp. Place duck on a rack over a baking tray and cook for 15–18 minutes. Slice duck and serve with salad greens.

Tarragon

Artemisia dracunculus

There are two commonly available forms of tarragon: the French (*Artemisia dracunculus*), which has a superior mild aniseed flavour; and the more vigorous growing Russian, with an inferior, bitter flavour that renders it a fairly useless herb for the culinary garden. French tarragon has mid-green, narrow long leaves and plants are lowish-growers to around 50cm/20in tall. Russian tarragon can reach up to 1.5m/5ft tall. Russian tarragon sets seed easily, and it's usually Russian tarragon which is sold as 'tarragon seed'. French tarragon rarely sets seed and is only sold as seedlings. We suggest you avoid Russian tarragon, and all following notes only apply to the preferred French tarragon.

Growing basics: tarragon likes full sun and well-drained soil. It needs protection from frosts in winter, but in milder, warmer climates it will die down partially in late winter, but a cutback and liquid feed in spring will bring it back to life. Liquid feed monthly in the growing season. Keep well watered on hot summer days. Plants will benefit from being lifted, divided and replanted every two to three years, to maintain vigour and flavour.

Growing in pots: French tarragon grows well in pots, but dividing and repotting clumps every two years maintains better growth and flavour.

Best time to sow: plant seedlings in spring or autumn. Tarragon can be grown from cuttings in late summer, and as the plant grows by sending out runners, sections of root can be taken and planted out to form new plants.

Picking tips: pick leaves fresh as needed.

In the kitchen: great with roast chicken, it also goes well with egg dishes, but it also combines very well with other herbs – along with chervil, chives and parsley, tarragon is a key ingredient in the classic French herb blend called 'fines herbes'.

Success secrets: get the right variety to start with; make sure to buy only French tarragon at the nursery. Look for labelled French tarragon seedlings, and don't use tarragon seed to grow plants as this seed is from the inferior Russian tarragon.

Heaven with: chicken, eggs, all vegetables, other herbs. For a change of flavour, try fresh tarragon instead of basil with tomatoes.

Oyster mushroom and walnut angel-hair salad

Serves 4

500g/1lb angel-hair pasta
½ cup olive oil
6 French shallots, chopped
200g/7oz oyster mushrooms
400g/14oz prosciutto, sliced
2 tablespoons pink or green peppercorns
2 tablespoons tarragon vinegar
4 tablespoons walnut oil
3 sprigs fresh tarragon
salt and freshly ground black pepper
75g/2½oz walnuts, chopped
½ cup pine nuts, roasted

1 Cook pasta in plenty of boiling salted water until tender but still firm to the bite. Drain and rinse with cold water. Pour a little oil through pasta to prevent it sticking together. Heat the remaining olive oil in a pan and sauté the shallots, oyster mushrooms and prosciutto for 3–4 minutes.

2 Add peppercorns and turn off heat.

3 Combine the vinegar, walnut oil, tarragon, salt, pepper and walnuts, and then toss through cooled pasta. Finally add in prosciutto, peppercorns and mushrooms, toss together and garnish with roasted pine nuts.

Tea

Camellia sinensis

While many herbs can be used to make a refreshing cup of tea, most of the tea consumed worldwide each year comes from a camellia bush, *Camellia sinensis*. Tea plantations are found in mountainous regions in tropical and subtropical zones (famously those in India, China and Sri Lanka), where temperatures are cooler yet also relatively consistent year-round. Though this is where the finest teas come from, *Camellia sinensis* will grow well in many climates, including temperate, frost-free areas.

Growing tips: C. sinensis will grow where other camellias grow successfully, although the tea obtained in all areas is not guaranteed for quality. Well-drained, fertile soil plus steady watering year-round are essential. The plant itself is a medium-sized tree to 17m/55ft tall in the wild, but which is pruned into a small (up to 2m/6ft) shrub for tea production. It has glossy green leaves and small white flowers with yellow stamens in spring. Tea plants are well suited to being grown as a clipped hedge in gardens. They like to grow in full sun or with some broken shade from mid-afternoon in summer.

Harvesting: it's the young top shoots from this evergreen shrub which are harvested for use in making tea, so you will need several plants to provide even a modest supply of tea leaves. This is why the clipped hedge is a good way to grow tea plants in the garden. They look good, and the regular clipping will produce the flushes of young new leaves needed for harvesting.

Tea types: green tea and black tea derive from the same plant, and the difference is in how the leaves are processed. In black tea, the leaves are fermented then dried, giving the leaves a longer shelf life. Green tea leaves are steamed (to prevent fermentation) then dried, and have a shorter shelf life. There are more than 3000 varieties of tea sold. Many are blends of different leaves, many are named after their region of origin (eg, Assam, Darjeeling, Ceylon, etc), and others have additional flavours added (eg, bergamot to make Earl Grey tea, and smoke to make Lapsang Souchong tea from Taiwan).

In the kitchen: as well as making cups of tea, you can use tea leaves to flavour a variety of sweet and savoury foods, from biscuits to cakes and ice-creams.

Medicinal benefits: tea is rich in anti-oxidant flavonoids and catechins, which help protect against harmful, cancer-causing free radicals. An average-strength cup of black tea has slightly less caffeine (50mg) than a similar-sized cup of instant coffee (60–70mg).

Thai lime

Citrus hystrix

This form of citrus, *Citrus hystrix*, is also known as the bai makrut lime in Thailand or the kaffir lime in Australia, UK and USA. It is a particularly fragrant plant whose leaves are as valuable as its fruits. This is a small-growing form of lime which can grow around 3m/10ft tall when mature, has unusual, highly fragrant double leaves which are joined at a narrow 'waist' in the middle. Its fruits are smallish, wrinkled and not very juicy, but they produce a superbly fragrant zest. Both the leaves and fruits are a key ingredient in Thai cookery.

Growing tips: Thai limes need the same growing conditions as other citrus varieties, namely plenty of sunshine, well-drained soil, regular feeding (in late winter and late summer) and watering, plus little competition from other plants growing inside its root zone. Though associated with tropical and subtropical regions, Thai limes will grow well in frost-free temperate climate zones. Take care with its position in the garden, as plants have sharp thorns, so don't grow it near the edge of paths or near doorways.

Growing in pots: Thai limes are especially well suited to growing in pots, one of the best citrus varieties for pots in fact. A minimum pot size of 40cm/16in diameter (measured across the top) is recommended, as are pot feet below the pot to ensure that excess water drains away. Slow-release fertilisers will provide the steady trickle of nutrients that potted citrus need. Potted Thai limes grow a bit smaller than in-ground trees, to just 1m/3ft tall.

In the kitchen: the leaves of Thai limes have many uses in Thai and other South-East Asian cuisines. After removing the thicker central rib from the leaves, they are usually finely sliced or chopped before being added to dishes, although whole leaves are tossed into soups and stocks. The fruits produce little juice, but the grated zest has a strong flavour similar to the leaves, which is especially useful in making salad dressings and dipping sauces. While it's is strongly associated with Thai cuisine, it's worth experimenting with it in any recipe where lime or lemon juice is needed. The leaves freeze very well, lasting up to a year. Fruits will last a number of weeks and can be stored in the fridge, in the same way as other citrus. Most people choose to leave the leathery leaves on their plates – but they can be eaten.

Tea potential: both the finely chopped leaves and the grated zest of Thai limes gives teas a wonderfully fragrant character all their own.

Thyme

Thymus vulgaris

Like sage and rosemary, thyme is another herb indigenous to the Mediterranean's shores. It's a low-growing, spreading herb that's available to herb gardeners in many varieties. The most common form, *Thymus vulgaris*, called garden thyme or common thyme, is a low, spreading shrub about 30cm/12in high, spreading to 50cm/20in or more, with small grey-green leaves and either white or pale lilac flowers in spring. Even within this one type of thyme, leaf widths can vary from narrow (French) to broad (English) types.

Growing basics: thyme loves full sunshine and well-drained soil and it will cope with dryness very well. It doesn't like excessively rich soils, so feed lightly. It's a very good rockery plant, spilling down rock or masonry surfaces. In areas with humid summers, which thyme doesn't like, growing it over rocks/bricks etc is a good way to lower humidity levels around plants.

Growing in pots: a wide shallow pot suits thyme best, one plant per pot. Feed with slow-release fertiliser in spring and let the potting mix dry out between waterings.

Best time to sow: sow seed in spring, summer or early autumn, but seedlings are readily available most of the year, and one plant is sufficient for most households' needs.

Picking tips: use scissors to snip a small bunch of stems when needed. Regular picking keeps plants bushier.

In the kitchen: older, woodier thicker stems are easier to work with in the kitchen, as you can 'zip' off a whole stem full of leaves between your thumb and forefinger, pulling down on sturdier old stems. Dried thyme is a useful herb, so if you have an excess dry it and store in a sealed jar.

Success secrets: regular picking keeps thyme plants bushier, but don't over-water plants.

Heaven with: many different soups, stews and casseroles it combines well with many vegetables, including broad beans, carrots, potatoes, tomatoes, corn and eggplant/aubergine.

Varieties: lemon thyme has a lemony tang that goes very well with chicken, veal or seafood; variegated thyme has yellow edges to leaves and a mild flavour; creeping thyme is mild-flavoured and grows as a creeper across the ground.

Za'atar: this Middle-Eastern herb is often included with thymes, even though it is in different genus (*Thymbra spicata*) as it is very thyme-like in flavour but in appearance it has longer leaves and is a woody shrub in gardens. Please note there is also a spice mixture called za'atar, which is made from za'atar thyme, sesame, sumac and salt.

Baked thyme-stuffed whole trout

Serves 4

1kg/36oz small new potatoes
¼ cup olive oil
4 small whole trout, scaled and cleaned
2 bunches thyme, washed and ends trimmed

1 Preheat the oven to 190°C/375°F.

2 Place the potatoes in a medium saucepan. Cover with cold water and bring to the boil. Cook for 5 minutes, then drain and place on a large baking tray. Pour over 4 tablespoons of the olive oil and toss to coat. Roast for 20–25 minutes until golden brown.

3 Meanwhile, tear off four pieces of aluminium foil large enough to wrap each trout. Score the trout 3 times on each side. Coat in the remaining oil and place onto the foil. Sprinkle a few thyme leaves over the fish and stuff the remaining thyme inside the cavity. Enclose the trout in the foil and place onto baking trays. Bake for 15–20 minutes until flesh flakes easily. Serve with the potatoes.

Turmeric

Curcuma longa

Along with galangal and ginger, turmeric is the third member of the ginger family to make a huge contribution to world cuisines, but turmeric, though harvested for its rhizomes (thick roots) is most familiar to cooks as a dry yellow powder, rather than as a fresh root. Turmeric (*Curcuma longa*, *C. domestica*) is a leafy tropical perennial 60–80cm/24–32in tall that produces clumps of attractive tropical-look broad green foliage. Its rhizomes are light brown on the outside and vividly orange inside.

Growing tips: turmeric is best suited to tropical zones with plenty of heat, humidity and rainfall, but it can be grown in the subtropics and frost-free, warm temperate areas (where it will die down in winter). Shop-bought fresh tubers are fine for planting. Well-drained soil and regular monthly fertilising will ensure good rhizome growth. In temperate areas, plant tubers 10-15cm deep in spring, once the weather warms. In tropical and subtropical zones, plant at any time, but water well in the dry season. A lightly-shaded position is best.

Growing in pots: turmeric can be grown in pots, but 40cm/16in across at the top is a recommended minimum size.

Harvesting: you can wait until the leaves yellow off at the end of the growing season before digging up plants for harvest, but you can also harvest individual rhizomes at any time. If harvesting whole plants, save some rhizomes for replanting.

In the kitchen: grated fresh turmeric has a sweet, nutty taste that is used in many dishes, including rice, casseroles, couscous, curries and stir-fries. The fresh leaves can also be used to wrap fish, chicken and other dishes before steaming. However, it's dried, powdered turmeric which is most used. Drying and processing turmeric at home isn't a practical option, so use shop-bought turmeric powder, which keeps well in an air-tight container for up to two years. Turmeric gives curry powders their yellow colour, and it's a key part of many spice mixes and pastes across many cuisines. Fresh turmeric rhizomes can be stored like ginger: wrap loosely in aluminium foil and keep it in the vegie crisper section of your fridge. It will usually last a few weeks.

Turmeric tea: recent research shows that turmeric may play a key role in preventing Alzheimer's disease, and in controlling cholesterol levels. To make turmeric tea, add 1 teaspoon turmeric powder to 1 cup boiling water. However, one cup a day is the max, and not every day either.

Monks butter bean salad

Serves 4

1 tablespoon sesame oil
1 tablespoon vegetable oil
2 cloves garlic, crushed
1 large onion, finely chopped
1 teaspoon ground turmeric
½ teaspoon chilli powder
½ teaspoon ground cardamom
2 x 300g/10oz canned butter beans, drained
¼ bunch fresh cilantro/coriander, chopped

1 Heat sesame and vegetable oils together in a wok over a medium heat, add garlic and onion and stir-fry for 5 minutes or until onion is soft.

2 Add turmeric, chilli powder and cardamom and stir-fry for 2 minutes longer or until fragrant.

3 Stir in beans and 1 cup of water and simmer for 15 minutes or until mixture thickens slightly. Sprinkle with coriander and serve immediately.

Valerian

Valeriana officinalis

This medicinal herb, native to Europe and Western Asia, has long been valued for the calming benefits provided by its roots, and research conducted in recent years backs that traditional belief. The plant itself is a 60–150cm/2–5ft tall perennial herb with hollow stems that produces white to pale pink flowers in summer. Its mid-green leaves have pronounced teeth along their edges.

Growing basics: valerian grows best in cool, dampish soil in positions ranging from full sun to part shade. It can be grown from seed sown direct in spring, or from plant divisions taken and replanted in spring or autumn. Plants should be cut back to remove finished flowers in late summer, to prevent self-seeding. Established plants can also be cut to the ground in late autumn, to reshoot in the following spring.

Growing in pots: valerian can be grown in pots, but diligent watering to keep soil damp is required.

Picking tips: it's the rhizomes which are harvested for medicinal uses. These are best taken in the plant's second or third year of growth, in late autumn, and used fresh or dried. Rhizomes are sliced into pieces before being air-dried.

In the kitchen: apart from making a cup of calming tea, valerian has few uses in the kitchen. However, extracts of valerian's essential oils are used in manufacturing various food products.

Medicinal benefits: while valerian has many claims made for its benefits, Dr Varro Tyler, in his book *Tyler's Honest Herbal* says valerian, at best, is a mild sedative. He also advises that a tea made from the fresh or dried roots is the best way to obtain the benefits offered by valerian, as the active ingredients found in extracts of valerian, offered in tablet form, tend to break down rapidly. There are claims that Valerian cures "restless legs" – a name for legs that move around during sleep at night. To make the 'tea', crush 1 teaspoon of dried root and soak in cold water overnight. Drink this tea as a mild sedative to ease insomnia or anxiety. However, it's not recommend that large doses of valerian tea be consumed for extended periods of time.

Rat bait: valerian roots have a distinctive, somewhat unpleasant smell (when dried, it's like stale sweat) which is known to be attractive to rats (and cats). For this reason valerian roots are often used as rat bait. In the famous children's folk tale, *The Pied Piper of Hamelin*, valerian is said to be the secret ingredient the Piper used to lure the rats away from the town.

Pictured right: Valerian can have pink or white flowers.

Vanilla

Vanilla planifolia

This popular flavouring comes from the processed, highly fragrant fruits of the vanilla orchid (*Vanilla planifolia*). Though they are referred to as vanilla 'beans' or 'pods' they are in fact classed as capsules. The plant itself is a perennial, climbing tropical orchid native to Mexico. It can reach 10–15m/33–50ft tall, has fleshy, bright green leaves 8–25cm/3–10in long and thrives in partial shade. The flowers are pale yellow-green and fragrant. Cultivation, and especially pollination of the flowers, is an intensive, hands-on process, and so vanilla is the world's second most expensive spice by weight, after saffron. Its main growing areas are Mexico, Madagascar, Reunion, Tahiti and Indonesia.

Growing tips: this tropical orchid needs expert cultivation to produce pods, and so it's not suited to amateur growers. Commercial growers are all located in the humid tropics, but orchids can be grown in greenhouses outside the tropics. The problem with growing vanilla orchids is that flowering is very brief, just a few hours on one day, and so all flowers must be hand-pollinated when they open. (In Mexico, pollination was originally done by a small bee, Melinopa, but this bee does not occur outside Mexico). If pollination is successful the flowers remain open for two to three days.

Harvesting: small capsules start appearing about six weeks after pollination and the capsules are harvested six to seven months later when the tips begin to turn yellow. Each capsule has to be harvested by hand as they don't all mature at the same time, so harvesting is carried out over a three-month period.

Curing: several more stages of processing are required before being ready for sale: these include fermentation, blanching, sweating then slow drying for a month. Finished pods are highly fragrant, dark brown, almost black, and wrinkled.

In the kitchen: vanilla is used to flavour many sweet dishes, including biscuits, custards, creams, yoghurt, cakes, sweets, ice-cream, liqueurs and fruit-based desserts. In many recipes the method is to cut a vanilla bean, scrape out the pulp and tiny seeds and add to the dish. Another method is to add a whole bean. A whole vanilla bean may be used up to four times: after cooking, remove it, wash and dry it and store in a sealed canister. One vanilla bean placed in a sugar canister will turn it into vanilla sugar, with a wide range of uses in making sweet dishes. Fresh beans can be kept in air-tight containers for up to two years.

Vanilla bean and white chocolate cheesecake

Serves 6–8

200g/7oz chocolate chip fudge or
   chocolate chip cookies
50g/1¾oz butter, melted
2 x 250g/9oz packets cream cheese
½ cup superfine/caster sugar
2 vanilla beans
3 teaspoons gelatine
¼ cup boiling water
300ml/10.5fl oz thickened cream, whipped
180g/6oz white chocolate, chopped

1 Break the cookies and place in a food processor. Process until the mixture resembles fine breadcrumbs. Place in a bowl and stir in the butter. Press the mixture into a 22cm/9in springform tin and place in the fridge to set for 30 minutes.

2 Beat the cream cheese and sugar together in a bowl.

3 Split the vanilla beans in half lengthways and scrape out the seeds using a sharp knife. Combine the seeds with the cream cheese and beat until the mixture is smooth.

4 Place the gelatine in a small bowl with the boiling water. Whisk until the gelatine dissolves. Leave for 2–3 minutes to cool.

5 Stir the cream and gelatine into the cream cheese mixture.

6 Place the chocolate in a small microwave dish. Microwave, uncovered, on medium heat for 1 minute, stir. Repeat the process in 30 second intervals until melted.

7 Stir the chocolate into the mixture and pour into the tin. Cover with plastic wrap and place in the fridge for 4–6 hours or overnight.

Note To dissolve gelatine in the microwave, combine water and gelatine in a small bowl. Microwave on high for 30 seconds or until dissolved.

Vietnamese mint

Polygonum odoratum syn. *Persicaria odoratum*

Known to the Vietnamese as rau ram, this herb also goes by the names of Vietnamese coriander and laksa leaf. Wherever Vietnamese migrants have journeyed, be it to the USA, Australia, France or elsewhere, they have taken this herb with them, as it's essential to their cuisine, and now it is an established part of herb gardens worldwide. Rau ram is not related to mint and gets this slightly misleading name because it grows like mint: low-growing, it spreads vigorously and thrives in any area with plentiful moisture, doing best in partial shade. The leaves themselves are mid-green, pointed with a distinctive dark marking around the middle of each leaf.

Growing basics: this is an easy herb to grow in a partially shaded spot in moist soil, so easy that it can become an invasive weed, just like mint. So, growing it in a wide, shallow pot is recommended. It grows best from any piece of the plant with a node on it – this will form roots in water within days. It doesn't like frosts at all, so is grown as a summer annual in cool climates, but can be grown year-round in frost-free warm temperate, subtropical and tropical zones. It's easy enough to strike a new plant from a piece bought as a fresh bunch sold by Asian food suppliers, although potted plants are becoming easier to find as the popularity of the plant grows.

Growing in pots: wide, shallow pots are the ideal way to grow this herb.

Harvest tips: pick young leaves as needed.

In the kitchen: the older these leaves become, the hotter and more peppery the flavour, so most cooks harvest the younger, milder leaves to use in cookery. Its uses in Vietnamese cookery are many, teaming especially well with fish and seafood, meat, poultry, and salad vegetables such as shredded cabbage, capsicums and bean sprouts. Thai cooks serve the leaves as a side dish with curries and traditional larb salads. On the Malay Peninsula, where it is called laksa leaf, it's a common garnish for the spicy coconut-milk infused fish, chicken or vegetable soup, laksa. You can use rau ram as a substitute for coriander in any cooked dish, but where coriander is used raw as a garnish, taste-test your rau ram leaves first, to make sure their hot and peppery flavour is not too strong.

Baked salmon

Serves 6–8

1.5kg/3.5lb whole salmon or ocean trout
1 tablespoon olive oil
2 teaspoons lime juice

Tomato Stuffing
2 vine-ripened tomatoes, diced
1 small red onion, diced
1 teaspoon lemon pepper seasoning
1/3 cup freshly chopped coriander
1/3 cup freshly chopped Vietnamese mint
1 tablespoon olive oil
1 tablespoon lime juice

1 To make the stuffing, combine the tomatoes, onion, lemon pepper seasoning, coriander, mint, olive oil and lime juice in a bowl. Set aside.

2 Preheat the oven to 180°C/350°F.

3 Rinse the salmon under cold water and pat dry with paper towel.

4 Combine the olive oil and lime juice in a small jug. Brush the salmon with oil and lime juice and place on a large piece of foil lined with baking paper.

5 Spoon the stuffing into the cavity and secure with toothpicks or a needle and thread.

6 Place on a baking tray and bake for 50–60 minutes or until cooked. It is best to have the salmon a little pink in the middle.

7 Unwrap the fish and remove the toothpicks or thread. Place on a serving plate and serve with crispy potatoes and salad.

Note To select whole fish, chose fish with clear, bulging eyes, firm flesh, red gills and shiny skin. To test if fish is cooked, insert a knife into the thickest part of the fish and gently divide to see if the flesh flakes. The flesh should come cleanly away from the backbone.

Wasabi

Wasabi japonica

Famous as the hot, pungent paste served in restaurants with Japanese sushi and sashimi, wasabi is a member of the brassica family which includes spicy horseradish and mustard, along with vegetables such as cabbages, cauliflower and broccoli. Wasabi (*Wasabi japonica* syn. *Eutrema wasabi*) grows naturally in mountain streams in Japan. Plants have a thick stem, long leaf stalks, glossy, deep-green, heart-shaped leaves and white flowers. Plants reach 40–60cm/16–24in tall, and the above-ground stem (not the root) is where the pungent flavour is most concentrated. In Japan, there are two basic grades of wasabi: the high quality 'sawa' wasabi, grown in semi-aquatic conditions, and the lesser 'oka' wasabi, grown in fields.

Growing tips: wasabi is not easy to grow at home, but if you are in a mountain area where temperatures are steadily cool (between 8–20°C/46–68°F) and you can provide the shade and constant moisture it prefers, it might be worth a go. Wherever ferns thrive, wasabi might also be able to grow.

In the kitchen: the very finely grated stem of the wasabi plant has an aromatic, hot yet sweet and pungent flavour. Once grated, this strong flavour doesn't last long (around 10-15 minutes is considered the maximum), and so it is best served fresh, grated at the table. The traditional Japanese grater is made from real sharkskin (called an 'oroshi'), but stainless steel graters are more common now. The grating process itself sets off a chemical reaction within the crushed cells that in turn produces the pungent flavour. Other parts of the wasabi plant, such as the leaves, do have a mild wasabi flavour and are mostly used as a garnish, but can be used in salads. As well as its well-known uses with raw fish and oysters, wasabi goes well in salad dressings and marries nicely with beef and rice dishes. Though often used on its own, it combines very well with ginger and soy sauce. In Japan, wasabi ice-cream is popular, as are wasabi flavoured nuts and other snacks. Like horseradish, wasabi doesn't retain its flavour when cooked.

Fake wasabi: most wasabi sold in shops as a powder in tins or a paste in tubes is not wasabi at all. It is a green coloured condiment made from horseradish, mustard and green colouring. In Japan this product (and horseradish itself) is sometimes referred to as 'western wasabi'.

Witch hazel

Hamamelis spp.

There's one outstanding reason why cooler climate gardeners like to grow witch hazel, and that's because in late autumn and winter its small but plentiful and extremely fragrant, spidery, golden-yellow flowers produce one of the best garden scents. The plant itself is a small, many-branched deciduous tree whose flowers appear on bare branches after the leaves have fallen in autumn. A native of North America, witch hazel is a shrub or small tree to around 4–5m/13–16ft tall, but there are now many cultivars and hybrids to choose from. The species used medicinally is *Hamamelis virginiana*, which isn't as spectacular in its flowering as some of the modern hybrids.

Growing basics: witch hazel does best in a cold, moist climate. It prefers a sheltered spot and is best bought and planted as grafted saplings in winter while dormant and bare-rooted.

Picking tips: leaves are picked and dried in summer for making medicines, and the bark is cut in spring, also for medical purposes.

In the kitchen: there are no uses for witch hazel in the kitchen.

Medicinal benefits: a traditional herbal medicine, the leaves and bark of the American species, *H. virginiana*, were originally used in a poultice designed to reduce inflammation in wounds and skin disorders. Later on the product was further processed and distilled into liquids called 'witch hazel water', although some were based on alcohol and others on water. These were applied externally to treat various skin conditions, such as eczema or burns, and when taken orally to treat varicose veins and hemorrhoids. Scientific tests have shown that it's the tannins in the bark and leaves which have a medicinal benefit. However, both 'witch hazel waters' are almost tannin-free, and very unlikely to be of any use. Dr Varro Tyler, in his book *Tyler's Honest Herbal* sadly concludes that "*Hamamelis* is so nearly destitute of medicinal virtues that it scarcely deserves official recognition." The only proven use of the alcohol-based witch hazel is as an astringent to treat hemorrhoids, but that benefit mostly comes from the alcohol, and not the witch hazel. The other prominent uses for witch hazel are in the cosmetics industry, especially in making skin treatments.

Divining rods: want to find water or gold? Witch hazel branches were the divining rod of choice in the pioneering days of the American settlers.

Wormwood

Artemisia absinthum

The notorious green-coloured alcoholic aperitif called absinthe, which was famed for its high alcohol content and mind-altering properties, was originally flavoured with wormwood. Most countries banned the making of absinthe in the early 20th century. Wormwood itself hasn't disappeared from the alcoholic drinks cabinet though, as it is still used to flavour vermouth (the name comes from the German name for wormwood, 'wermut'). Wormwood is one of the most bitter herbs grown (the species name '*absinthum*' means 'without sweetness'), and its traditional uses included deterring household pests such as moths and fleas. The plant itself is an evergreen perennial 1m/3ft tall which is mostly a foliage plant with attractive grey-green leaves, although it does produce sprays of tiny yellow flowers in summer.

Growing basics: wormwood can be grown from its extremely fine seed, by taking cuttings, or lifting, dividing and replanting established clumps in spring or autumn. This plant does best in light, well-drained soils and full sun. Prune back plants every year in autumn, once flowering finishes. It is fairly frost-hardy, but in severely cold winter climates it might need protection from deep frosts.

Growing in pots: wormwood can be grown in large pots.

Picking tips: flowers and leaves are harvested for drying, just as the flowers begin to open. They are then air-dried, for uses in the house such as repelling moths, fleas and other pests. After drying, it is also sometimes added to vinegar, to be used as an antiseptic cleaner around the house.

In the kitchen: wormwood has no culinary uses – indeed, see below for tips on why consuming this herb could be hazardous to health.

Medicinal benefits: in his book *The Honest Herbal*, Dr Varro Tyler says the mind-altering reputation of wormwood is due to the presence of the chemical thujone in its volatile oils. Its chemical mechanism is thought to work on the same brain receptors affected by the chemical THC when it's ingested while consuming marijuana. The other proven medical use for wormwood is that of treating worms in the digestive tract. However, due to the dangers of taking wormwood, Dr Tyler concludes that it "has no place in modern phytomedicine" ie, plant-based medicine, and it shouldn't be ingested as a form of self-medication.

Yarrow

Achillea millefolium

Related to chamomile (*Chamaemelum nobile*, *Matricaria recutita*), yarrow is a useful medicinal herb (as is chamomile) whose summer flowers add colour to a herb garden. However, the plant itself grows so easily it is weedy, and it is often also seen growing as a weed in waste ground and pastures. It's a 30–90cm/1–3ft tall perennial with dark green, very fine, feathery, aromatic leaves and is covered in clusters of tiny, pink-tinged white flowers in summer and autumn. It's an ancient healing herb that gets its genus name, *Achillea*, from the legendary Ancient Greek warrior Achilles, who, in Homer's epic poem, *The Iliad*, used this herb to heal wounds.

Growing basics: yarrow grows so well in conditions it likes that your main task will be to stop its spread, as it is very weedy by nature. The easiest way to get started is to lift, divide and replant a section from an existing clump, or to plant a seedling, in spring or early autumn. It can also be grown from seed, but germination is erratic. It does best in well-drained soil in full sun in temperate and cool climates, and is a very winter-hardy plant. To stop its spread, cut off flower heads when flowering fades, to prevent seed forming.

Growing in pots: yarrow has a creeping rootstock which makes it hard to contain inside a pot, so it's not a good choice for pots.

Picking tips: both the leaves and flowers are harvested at the beginning of its flowering season.

In the kitchen: yarrow has few uses in the kitchen, although its young, tender leaves are edible and a few can be tossed into a mixed garden salad. However, eat it only occasionally, as too much is known to cause skin irritations.

Medicinal benefits: the two closely plants, chamomile and yarrow, have many used in herbal medicine that scientific research has proven to be valid. Yarrow is a carminative (ie, aids digestion and prevents flatulence) and it also has uses as an anti-inflammatory, anti-spasmodic and anti-infective agent.

Yarrow tea: yarrow makes a soothing, gently medicinal cup of tea, Pour 1 cup boiling water over ¼ cup of fresh yarrow leaves and flowers, let it steep 5 minutes, then strain and pour. You can also use cooled yarrow tea as a wash to speed the healing of minor cuts and grazes. However, do not drink yarrow tea regularly, keep it occasional at best.

Index of scientific names

Achillea millefolium 300
Agastache foeniculum 144
Agastache rugosa 144
Allium sativum 128
Allium schoenoprasum 74
Allium tuberosum 74
Aloe barbadensis (see
    Aloe vera) 22
Aloe vera 22
Aloysia citriodora 156
Alpinia galanga 124
Alpinia officinarium 124
Amaranthus
    leucocarpus 24
Amaranthus caudatus 24
Amaranthus dubins 24
Amaranthus oleraceus 24
Amaranthus retroflexus 24
Amaranthus spinosus 24
Amaranthus spp. 24
Amaranthus tricolor 24
Anethum graveolens 112
Anthriscus cerefolium 62
Apium graveolens
    var. dulce 56
Armoracia rusticana 140
Artemisia absinthum 298
Artemisia dracunculus 268
Atriplex hortensis 58

Backhousia citriodora 154
Barbarea verna 98
Basella alba 58
Borago officinalis 40
Brassica alba 170
Brassica juncea 170
Brassica nigra 170
Brassica rapa var.
    nippisinica 58
Brassica spp. 170

Calendula 162
Camellia sinensis 272
Capparis decidua 42
Capparis inermis 42
Capparis spinosa 42
Capparis spp. 42
Capsicum annuum 192

Capsicum annuum 70
Capsicum frutescens 70
Carum carvi 46
Centaurea cyanus 96
Chamaemelum nobile 60
Cichorium intybus 68
Cinnamomum verum 78
Citrus hystrix 274
Citrus spp. 82
Corchorus olitorius 58
Coriandrum sativum 92
Crocus sativus 228
Cuminum cyminum 102
Curcuma domestica 280
Curcuma longa 280
Cymbopogon citratus 150

Diplotaxis erucoides 218
Diplotaxis muralis 218

Echinacea angustifolia 116
Echinacea purpurea 116
Elettaria cardamomum 50
Eruca vesicaria
    ssp. sativa 218

Foeniculum vulgare 118
Foeniculum vulgare var.
    azoricum 118

Ginkgo biloba 136
Glycyrrhiza glabra 158

Hamamelis spp. 296
Hamamelis virginiana 296
Helianthus annuus 262
Hypericum perforatum 254

Illicium verum 256

Juniperus communis 142

Lactuca sativa 236
Laurus nobilis 36
Lavandula angustifolia 146
Lavandula dentata 146
Lavandula stoechas 146
Lepidium sativum 98

Levisticum officinale 160
Limnophila aromatica 216

Mangifera indica 26
Matricaria recutita 60
Melissa officinalis 148
Mentha spicata 164
Murraya koenigii 106
Musa x paradisiaca 30
Myristica fragrans 182

Nasturtium officinale (see
    also Tropaeolum
    majus) 98
Nepeta cataria 54
Nepeta faassenii 54
Nigella damascena 178
Nigella sativa 178

Ocimum basilicum 32
Origanum majorana 186
Origanum vulgare 186

Panax ginseng 138
Panax pseudoginseng 138
Panax quinquefolius 138
Pandanus
    amaryllifolius 190
Pandanus tectorius 190
Papaver somniferum 210
Pelargonium
    graveolens 240
Pelargonium crispum 240
Pelargonium spp. 240
Perilla frutescens 204
Petroselinum crispum 196
Pimenta dioica 18
Piper nigrum 200
Polygonum odoratum
    syn. Persicaria
    odoratum 290
Punica granatum 206

Rhus coriaria 258
Rosa canina 226
Rosa cvs. 226
Rosa damascena 226
Rosa rugosa 226

Rosmarinus officinalis 222
Rumex acetosa 250
Rumex scutatus 250
Rumex spp. 250

Salvia officinalis 232
Satureja spp. 238
Sesamum orientale 242
Stellaria media 66
Symphytum officinale 90
Syzygium aromaticum 86

Tagetes 162
Tamarindus indica 264
Tanacetum
    cinerariifolium 214
Tanacetum
    parthenium (former
    Chrysanthemum
    parthenium) 122
Taraxacum officinale 110
Tasmannia lanceolata 168
Tetragonia
    tetragonioides 58
Thymus vulgaris 276
Trigonella foenum-
    graecum 120
Tropaeolum majus 172
Tropaeolum majus (see
    also Nasturtium
    officinale) 98

Urtica dioica 176
Urtica spp. 176

Valeriana officinalis 284
Valerianella locusta 236
Vanilla planifolia 286

Wasabi japonica 294

Zanthoxylum
    piperitum 246
Zanthoxylum simulans 246
Zingiber officinale 132

Index of common names

Allspice 18
Aloe vera 22
Amaranthus 24
Amchoor 26

Bananas 30
Basil 32
Bay leaf 36
Borage 40

Caperberries 42
Capers 42
Caraway 46
Cardamom 50
Catmint 54
Catnip 54
Celery leaf 56
Ceylon spinach 58
Chamomile 60
Chervil 62
Chickweed 66
Chicory 68
Chillies 70
Chives 74
Cinnamon 78
Citrus 82
Cloves 86
Comfrey 90
Coriander (seed & leaf) 92
Cornflowers 96
Cress 98
Cumin 102
Curry leaf 106

Dandelion 110
Dill 112

Echinacea 116

Fennel 118
Fenugreek 120
Feverfew 122

Galangal 124

Garlic 128
Garlic chives 74
Ginger 132
Ginkgo 136
Ginseng 138

Horseradish 140

Juniper 142

Korean mint 144

Lavender, English 146
Lemon balm 148
Lemon grass 150
Lemon myrtle 154
Lemon verbena 156
Licorice 158
Lovage 160

Mace 182
Marigolds 162
Marjoram 186
Mint 164
Mountain pepper 168
Mustard 170

Nasturtium 172
Nettle 176
Nigella 178
Nutmeg 182

Oregano 186

Pandan 190
Paprika 192
Parsley 196
Pepper 200
Perilla 204
Pomegranate 206
Poppy 210
Pyrethrum 214

Rice paddy herb 216

Rocket 218
Rosehips 226
Rosemary 222
Roses 226

Saffron 228
Sage 232
Salad herbs 236
Savory 238
Scented geraniums 240
Sesame 242
Sichuan pepper 246
Sorrel 250
St John's wort 254
Star anise 256
Sumac 258
Sunflower 262

Tamarind 264
Tarragon 268
Tea 272
Thai lime 274
Thyme 276
Turmeric 280

Valerian 284
Vanilla 286
Vietnamese mint 290

Wasabi 294
Witch hazel 296
Wormwood 298

Yarrow 300

Index of recipes

Apple and Cinnamon Cupcakes	80
Aromatic Lemon Roast Chicken	130
Asian Greens with Sweet Soy and Sesame Dressing	244
Asparagus, Ricotta and Herb Frittata	76
Baby Octopus Marinated in Olive Oil and Oregano	188
Baby Spinach Tarts	184
Baked Apples	20
Baked Salmon	292
Baked Spiced Pears	52
Baked Thyme-stuffed Whole Trout	278
Beef Keema	134
Beef Pho	94
Beef Rendang	152
Bitki with Dill Sauce	114
Blue Cheese and Onion Quiche	48
Bombay Hot Lentils	108
Bruschetta with Tomato and Basil	34
Calamari in Garlic and Capers	44
Chicken and Coconut Soup	126
Chicken Jambalaya	38
Chilli Crab	72
Citrus Meringue Pie	84
Crab Rice Paper Rolls	166
Crayfish with Green Herbs	64
Crispy Fried Duck	266
Delicious Bouillabaisse	230
Grilled Sumac Fish	260
Hungarian Goulash Soup	194
Lemon Poppy Cupcakes	212
Monks Butter Bean Salad	282
Oyster Mushroom and Walnut Angel-Hair Salad	270
Pomegranate Exotica	208
Pork and Sage-Filled Ravioli	234
Pork Fillet with Rocket, Apple and Parmesan Salad	220
Risotto Niçoise	198
Roast Potatoes with Garlic and Rosemary	224
Seared Tuna Salad with Crisp Wontons	180
Sichuan Beef Stir-Fry	248
Smoked Chicken Pappardelle with Nasturtium Butter	174
Sorrel Soup	252
Sour Prawn (Shrimp) Curry	28
Stout-Glazed Ham	88
Sultana Orange Chicken	202
Tikka Skewers	104
Vanilla Bean and White Chocolate Cheesecake	288
Watercress and Apple Salad	100